LORD *of the* RAMS

THE GREATEST STORY NEVER TOLD

Orla,
with Best wishes.
Ronan 29-8-08.

RONAN SMITH

Trafford
PUBLISHING™

www.trafford.com

North America & international
toll-free: 1 888 232 4444 (USA & Canada)
phone: 250 383 6864 ♦ fax: 250 383 6804
email: info@trafford.com

The United Kingdom & Europe
phone: +44 (0)1865 722 113 ♦ local rate: 0845 230 9601
facsimile: +44 (0)1865 722 868 ♦ email: info.uk@trafford.com

10 9 8 7 6 5 4 3 2 1

To my parents James and Nuala

Acknowledgements

The writing of *Lord of the Rams* has been a laboured and time-consuming yet ultimately rewarding and enriching experience. But behind my obvious role on this project, there are those who have provided the final 'spit and polish', those who have offered advice and encouragement, and those who—by their very existence—have inspired me to tell my story.

I would like to thank Glen and Deirdre McArdle; Glen for his splendid work on the book cover and Deirdre for her professional editing of the final manuscript. A great tag team effort to be sure!

Special thanks to John Geary for his invaluable advice and insightful input, which was much appreciated.

Thanks to Keith Geraghty, Gavin O'Dowd, Derek Stanley and Sean Mara for reviewing early drafts of the book and for their generous feedback, which encouraged me throughout the long four-year gestation period.

I'd also like to express my sincere gratitude to the many people who have weighed in with suggestions during the 'creative process' and to those whose anecdotes and recollections have helped jog my memory. In particular, thanks again to Keith, Gavin, Derek and Sean. Thanks also to Stephen Gammell, Pauric and Eugene Tighe, and Martin Brady. And thanks to Colmán McLaughlin for 'Word of the Day' and to my family for their unconditional love and support.

Finally, thanks to those who have inspired me to write this book, particularly my many lifelong friends from Munterconnaught and Oldcastle. My life is richer for knowing each and every one of you, and this book is my way of saying thanks – for the friendships, the fun and the laughter.

Contents

Introduction   7

Chapter 1 – From Dublin to Munterconnaught   9

Chapter 2 – Little Devils   14

Chapter 3 – 100 Lines for 100 Crimes   19

Chapter 4 – Pranks and Pets   26

Chapter 5 – Wrestling with Cider   31

Chapter 6 – The Painmaster   37

Chapter 7 – Raymond, Ronan and Red Cards   44

Chapter 8 – It Doesn't Always Rain in Mayo   48

Chapter 9 – Dancing, Turning, Picking   54

Chapter 10 – Shame on you, Ray Houghton   60

Chapter 11 – A New and Mature Rams   64

Chapter 12 – Get Out, Stay Out and Get the Fire Brigade Out   71

Chapter 13 – Fate Takes Over   79

Chapter 14 – It's a Long Way from Munterconnaught   84

Chapter 15 – Turning the Water into Wine   89

Chapter 16 – No Pain, No Shame, No Brains   95

Chapter 17 – New Faces from Strange Places   103

Chapter 18 – The Fall of the House of Munchies   110

Chapter 19 – Hide and Seek   116

Chapter 20 – The Height of Stupidity, The Depths of Despair   122

Chapter 21 – Hard Times at Flat 4A   129

Chapter 22 – The Stalker   135

Chapter 23 – Not a Typical Weekend   142

Chapter 24 – Exam Time   147

Chapter 25 – The Trouble with Fishing, Dublin and Discos   154

Chapter 26 – An Odjous New Job   163

Chapter 27 – A Place to Call 'Home'   168

Chapter 28 – London's Calling   175

Chapter 29 – The Season of Good Will   183

Chapter 30 – The Rattlin' Bog   189

Chapter 31 – New York, New York   194

Chapter 32 – Munterconnaught's Other Sons   201

Chapter 33 – Back to New York   209

Chapter 34 – Where Everybody Knows Your Name   218

INTRODUCTION

'**G**ROW UP a few years,' a teacher once said to me many years ago. Had I heeded him, the book you're about to read would be very short indeed. Instead, I replied a split-second later with a smart-assed reply, which was typical of my laidback, juvenile personality.

'In a few years,' I said, and I continued acting the fool. If truth be known, it wasn't really yours truly who was misbehaving. The blame could be placed squarely on the shoulders of 'the Rams'. Let me explain.

The name 'Rams' was short for 'Rambo', which in turn was short for 'Randy Rambo' - a nickname I had being blessed with since the early days of my youth when my peers knew little of the meaning of the word 'randy'.

Not content with just one nickname, I tailored the name Rambo into a longer word—Ramsmobile. That name didn't mean anything whatsoever, but there was a euphonious ring to it. And soon I began referring to myself in the third person—as you do.

'The Man of Steel, The Ramsmobile, The Lean Machine,' I would holler. Over the years I've often referred to myself by other names such as 'The Painmaster', 'No Pain' and 'Lord of the Rams', but most people have come to know me simply as 'Rams', 'the Rams' or 'Rambo'.

My Rams persona has effectively served as my alter ego for most of my life. Ronan is naturally shy, polite and a true gentleman. Rams, on the other hand, is boisterous, outgoing, politically incorrect, quick-witted and slightly unstable.

Ronan appears at family get-togethers, boardroom meetings and anywhere else where good manners are expected. The Rams, however, can appear anywhere at any time and—as you'll soon discover—he's capable of doing just about anything.

Throughout this book, you'll read about some of the adventures from the first 25 years of Rams's life. You'll meet some of his closest and most eccentric friends, and you'll probably wonder whether any of them will, 'grow up a few years'.

Hopefully you'll have a good time finding out.

Ronan Smith
27 January 2008

Chapter 1

FROM DUBLIN TO MUNTERCONNAUGHT

E VER MEET somebody and think, 'That guy's mad in the head'? Well, many people have thought that upon meeting the Rams for the first time, and maybe they were correct—to some degree. His mother always attributed his 'unique' personality to the time his oldest sister, Vanessa, pushed him down a flight of stairs when he was just two years of age. On closer examination, however, he appeared to be no different to the many colourful people who surrounded him in the tiny parish of Munterconnaught in Co. Cavan.

The Rams was born in the Coombe hospital in Dublin in 1978, living in Rathmines for the first two years of his life. His memories from those city days were practically non-existent, although his mother, Nuala, had plenty of stories from that time. Her favourite served as a lesson in how not to address the first black person you ever meet; in this case a middle-aged woman who was queuing behind her in a grocery shop in Rathmines. Standing beside his mother, Rams stared in amazement at a woman unlike he had ever seen before. He pointed at her and tried to get his mother's attention, but she failed to notice because she was busy trying to pay for her groceries. Well he wanted answers and he wanted them now. All at once, a tiny voice silenced everyone in the queue.

'Mammy, Mammy. Why is that woman covered in chocolate?'

One rushed and embarrassed apology later and Mrs. Smith and her son were out of that particular shop, never to return. Even at that

9

tender age, albeit inadvertently on that occasion, the Rams was showing the signs of being somewhat of a loose-tongued smart ass, and boy
was he in good company in Munterconnaught, a place he would find
himself moving to just a few weeks after the 'Chocolate Incident'.

Munterconnaught was the tiniest of rural communities, where
there was little to do and plenty of time in which to do it. The focal
point of the parish was undoubtedly the shop, Boylan's, which was
attached to a pub of the same name and was across the road from
the football field and clubrooms. A further mile down the road was
Knocktemple National School, and it was there that the Rams started
his adventures.

Three years after moving to Munterconnaught, the Rams enrolled
as a pupil at the primary school. It was a tiny building with just three
classrooms, three teachers and two or three classes in each classroom.
As he entered his classroom for the first time, he couldn't help but
notice numerous toy-laden tables lining the walls along each side of
the room. At first, he thought he'd arrived at a massive toy store, but
he soon discovered that strict rules forbade the children from playing
with the toys.

It was lunchtime and across the room from the Rams sat another
boy of the same age who was also experiencing his first day at school.
His name was Keith Geraghty and, unlike the Rams, he had brought a
few toys to school with which to pass the time. But the teacher, Mrs.
McMahon, took a bit of a shine to Keith's farmyard animals, and it
wasn't long before they were sitting proudly amongst her other col-
lectibles. As it happened, Keith wasn't in the habit of sharing his toys
with middle-aged women, and shortly thereafter he reclaimed them
on behalf of every four and a half year old who has ever had his toys
confiscated.

Unfortunately, Keith's actions didn't amuse McMahon who forced
him to surrender his toys or face the wrath of her almighty 30-inch
ruler. Over the next few days the two boys gradually smuggled Keith's
prized possessions from McMahon's Alcatraz-like mountain of toys
and, in the process of doing so, formed the foundations of what would
become a long-standing friendship.

Keith lived about half a mile away from the school and always walked home afterwards with his brothers while the Rams made the journey home on a bus that wasn't fit to carry farm animals. The four Geraghty brothers would often be seen eating gooseberries off the bushes on their way home and, as a result, Keith's brother, Trevor, soon picked up the nickname Goosey. Eventually Keith also earned the same nickname but, unlike Trevor, the name stuck with him for life.

A few weeks into the school year the baby infants' class was complete. Rams, Goosey, seven girls and another boy, Derek Stanley, made up a bigger than average class in a smaller than average school. Amongst the boys, it was common practice to refer to one's mates by their surname, and so Derek soon became known as Stanley, then as Stan the Man and eventually just Stano. Being the only boys in the class, the three quickly became great friends.

Mrs. McMahon taught the two infant classes in the school and, following the obligatory two-year stretch, the boys found themselves in Miss Plunkett's class where they would spend the next three years of their education. It was during these formative years that the Rams would start showing signs of being too smart for his own good, which meant that he wasn't always popular with people in authority.

Typically, Plunkett would be telling a story or attempting to teach a lesson when the Rams would give his 10 cents' worth, finishing her sentences with comments that would leave her speechless.

Plunkett was a young teacher in her early twenties and had probably never been trained in college to deal with the anecdotes of an eight year old boy who could have out-talked politicians. Usually, she would accept defeat and laugh along with the rest of the class. A common way of dealing with pupils who continuously talked out of turn was to ask them if they wanted to teach the class, and this would always result in them falling silent, thereby handing the victory to the teacher. But one day, while the Rams was being particularly smart-assed, Plunkett made the fatal mistake of asking him the question he'd been waiting for.

'You seem to know it all. Why don't you come up here and teach the class if you think you're so smart?'

'Ah sure I'll give it a go,' quipped the Rams, face beaming.

Plunkett looked slightly fazed to see him approaching the top of the class so confidently, but she quietly took a seat in the corner of the room, feeling somewhat safe in the knowledge that he would surely fall flat on his face and embarrass himself in front of the entire class. But the Rams was out to prove that he was more than capable of teaching a group of 7-10 year olds. Sure how tough could it be?

Rams grabbed a piece of chalk and proceeded with the Mathematics class he had rudely interrupted just moments earlier. Initially, the rest of the pupils fell quiet but, as the Rams grew in confidence and claimed ownership of the blackboard, they began to revel in his unique method of teaching. For the next five minutes he called up Goosey, Stano and some of the younger lads from the class below him to complete some of the problems Plunkett had chalked onto the board prior to the 'takeover'. Once completed, the Rams decided to take questions from the audience as Plunkett looked on, her lower jaw almost hitting the ground. The last question came from Paul McGovern who, like everyone else, was enjoying Rams's unorthodox method of teaching.

'An bhfuil cead agam dul amach go dtí an leithreas mas é do thoil é?' he said in Irish, which was mandatory at school in order for students to gain permission to use the toilet.

As was always the case, the Rams needed little more than a millisecond to compose an answer.

'No, you can piss in your trousers.'

The class erupted into laughter, but Miss Plunkett could take no more. She burst into tears and ran out of the class for the safe confines of the staff room. Suddenly the laughter came to an abrupt end and one or two of the pupils, fearing reprehension upon her return, begged the Rams to rectify the situation. For once, he felt that he may have over-stepped the mark, and he knew he had to act quickly before Mrs. McMahon, or worse still, the headmaster Declan Cooney, found Plunkett crying in the staff room. Five minutes of apologising put everything straight and the pair returned to class. The Rams tightened the reins on his mouth for the remainder of the day and Plunkett—unsurprisingly—never asked anyone to teach the class again.

Chapter 2

LITTLE DEVILS

LIKE MANY other rural areas in the 1980s, Munterconnaught didn't have much to offer the local kids in terms of amenities that might keep them off the streets. Therefore, Gaelic football became an important part of life for the boys from an early age, and camogie served as the sport of choice for the girls.

Rams, Goosey and Stano were 10 when they started turning up for training for the under-14 football team, which had enjoyed some success over the years. Rams loved the football and his occasional stints in goal, but it was the evening trips to other parishes for away matches, and the accompanying craic on the bus, that he most looked forward to.

By now, the boys had moved into the headmaster's classroom where, over the course of the next three years, they would complete their primary school education. Declan Cooney was a reasonably strict but fair and well-liked principal. He also had a great interest in Gaelic and—weather prevailing—he would bring the boys out for a game once a week. He would pick two teams and then play along-side one of them. It didn't seem fair to the Rams that a grown man could be on one team whereas the other team would have to make do with players who were barely five foot tall. Fortunately, there was a great equaliser of sorts who went by the name of Mark McGovern. McGovern was in the class above the Rams. He was of average height for his age but had strength well beyond his years. Rams

often wondered if McGovern was on a diet of angel dust and ste-
roids instead of porridge and spuds like everyone else, such was the
difference in strength between him and everyone he encountered.

As it happened, McGovern was also the best footballer in the school
at that time, so Cooney would always play on the opposite team
to him in an attempt to keep the teams evenly matched. Cooney's
size advantage allowed him to easily knock most of the lads off the
ball but the enthusiastic headmaster didn't fare as well when facing
McGovern. The two would always mark each other and, at least once
in every match, McGovern would run at Cooney, hitting him with a
shoulder and tripping him to the ground. He would then grab the ball
from him and run up the field to score a point or goal. The sight of
an eleven year old boy knocking lumps out of the headmaster would
have the rest of the class in stitches every time. McGovern would always claim the 'unfortunate trip' was accidental and Cooney, being
somewhat gullible, would believe him.

McGovern was also a little devil when he had the ball in his possession. Sometimes, rather than looking to see where the goalposts were,
he'd have a look to see where Cooney was located and, after spotting
him, he'd kick the ball as hard as he could towards the unsuspecting headmaster, always just missing his head by mere inches. Such
unusual antics would liven up any game of Gaelic, but McGovern
had yet more tricks up his sleeve when left to his own devices at
lunchtime.

The 'old school' stood on the same plot of land as Knocktemple
National School. It closed in 1971, and shortly thereafter the new
school opened behind it. Nevertheless, the old school had a certain
charm about it, which made it a popular vehicle of sorts around which
the kids would play. For one thing, playing around the front of the old
school meant that the teachers, while dining in the staff room of the
'new school', couldn't see what the kids were up to. Part of the old
school roof was flat and, by climbing the drainpipes, the boys had a
good hiding place from the teachers if all hell broke loose, as it often
did. Piggyback fighting, football and the occasional fistfight would
go on in front of the school unbeknownst to the teachers. There was

also a new and unique game invented by none other than McGovern.

Unsurprisingly, McGovern's game involved the use of a football. While playing Gaelic unsupervised at lunchtime, he would occasionally aim the ball at the nearest window of the old school. Bang—broken pane of glass. He would then go to the staff room and tell Cooney that he had 'accidentally' smashed a window; Cooney would tell him it was okay and to be more careful in future, and eventually this became a weekly routine with McGovern always walking away smelling of roses for being 'brave enough' to own up to the breakage.

The rest of the lads were mystified as to how McGovern was never disciplined, so one day they decided they'd all have a go. The old school windows each consisted of 12 square panes of glass and the chance of two panes breaking in the one window on the same day was such that it would surely arouse suspicion from Cooney. Nonetheless, the lads would try their best to test his patience to its limits. Anthony Dunne was the first to step up to the plate. He was in the same class as McGovern, as was Gavin O'Dowd who put the second pane of glass through, followed by Goosey, Stano and finally the Rams. With five panes broken, the lads went to Cooney in five-minute intervals to explain their respective 'accidents'. By the time the Rams half-laughingly told Cooney, 'There's been a bit of an accident', there was steam coming out of the poor headmaster's ears. The ball was confiscated and the lads were told they would have to pay for the damages. Cooney eventually let them away without having to pay anything, but they had learned a valuable lesson—if they wanted to break windows in the future and get away with it, then McGovern was the only man for the job.

Cooney may have won that particular battle but he was never likely to win the war if the Rams and his mates had their way. Christmas was coming, and they knew it was the perfect time for giving.

By now, Goosey was emerging as a bit of a prankster. He was always pulling tricks or performing gross acts such as picking up cow's shite and running it through his fingers. He lived on a farm and the 'shite handling' was one of his party pieces whenever Rams and Stano would visit. The lads might be helping to herd a few cattle into one of the fields when Goosey would spring into action. Just to make it even grosser, he would normally pick up a cowpat that looked like it had been sitting on the grass for six months, was green, rock hard on the outside and covered with flies. Apparently, his reason for doing so was to prove that he wasn't afraid to get his hands dirty, and he definitely proved his point.

Despite Goosey's jester-like antics, the Rams wasn't in any way suspicious when the prankster arrived into class shortly before the Christmas break with a carefully-wrapped gift for him. The two lads, along with Stano, would normally exchange gifts every Christmas, so this act wasn't out of the ordinary. Unwrapping the gift, Rams was surprised to see a large box of sweets before him. He knew that if he opened it in class, the vultures would devour the goods within minutes, so he opted to put the box into his schoolbag. It was still break-time so Cooney was busy finishing his tea in the staff room, creating the perfect opportunity for Paul McGovern to sneak over to the schoolbag and tear a gaping hole in the box. Before the Rams had a chance to react, he could see the contents of the box tumbling out of the hole and, rather than sweets, big stones crash-landed onto the floor with a thud.

Unbeknownst to the Rams, almost everyone in the class had been in on Goosey's prank and—by refusing to share his gift— the Rams had unwittingly deflated the air from Goosey's cunningly-conceived plan. As a last resort, and as a means of evoking some sort of response from the mean Cavan bastard, Paul had decided to open the box, thereby revealing the truth. Unfortunately, the trick had by now been severely diluted and thus didn't deliver the laughs that Goosey had expected.

Nonetheless, the raw ingredients for a prank and a half were lying on the floor, and Goosey knew he had to act fast. Gathering up the stones, he placed them back in the box in such a way that picking it up would once again relieve it of its contents. This time, however, he placed the time bomb in the middle of Cooney's desk and returned to his seat just as his unsuspecting victim returned to the classroom.

A big smile that would put the Mona Lisa to shame lit up Cooney's face. For months he had been terrorised by these kids who did their utmost to make his life hell and now with Christmas approaching he realised that perhaps these little devils might not be on the one-way street to Hell.

'Ah guys, I don't believe it,' he said, approaching the desk and gleefully reaching for the box. 'Thanks very much. There was no need for this at al...'

As stones cascaded onto his desk, cutting him off mid-sentence, Cooney quickly realised that he had been duped by the same shower of heartless bastards who he—almost for a fraction of a second—believed might have changed their ways. Dumping the stones into the bin, he set the class some exercises, but the reborn devils failed miserably to contain their laughter. Happy Christmas indeed!

Chapter 3

100 LINES FOR 100 CRIMES

CONTRARY TO what Cooney might have thought, the war being waged in the classroom against him wasn't personal. But children will be children, and many of Muntercon-naught's offspring would have stretched anyone's patience. Cooney's main method of disciplining them involved issuing 'lines'. This entailed the offender having to write, 'I will not misbehave in class', or similar, into a copybook a set number of times.

'100 lines,' Cooney would roar across the classroom whenever someone misbehaved. 100 lines seemed to be sufficient punishment for 90 percent of offences, including talking in class, laughing out loud in class and—for those asking for trouble—farting in class.

The Rams didn't perceive Cooney's disciplinary methods to be too harsh. A few years earlier students around the country might have been expected to go outside, fell a fully-grown tree with their bare hands, and drag it into the classroom so that the headmaster could, with considerable pleasure, beat them over the arse with it in front of all their school friends. So, by comparison, writing 100 short lines on a sheet of paper wasn't exactly the end of the world.

200 lines were occasionally issued to repeat offenders or to those guilty of more serious misdemeanours such as hiding Cooney's chair or chalking a rude drawing onto the blackboard. Pauric Tighe was one of the most frequent recipients of this punishment. He was even louder than, and at times just as cheeky as, the Rams. His gruff

accent proved to be quite distinguishable from his classmates and this often led to him being correctly penalised by the headmaster for various crimes.

One such example occurred during singing class, which was held every now and again by Breeda McMahon. Breeda, who was Mrs. McMahon's daughter and an avid singer and musician, had recently commenced teaching at the school in the same classroom that had been occupied by Miss Plunkett just a couple of years earlier. Given Breeda's penchant for the harp, organ, and traditional music and hymns, it wasn't long before she had informally arranged to take Cooney's class for the occasional singing lesson, where she would provide the music and the children would—in theory at least—provide the dulcet harmonies.

Breeda, however, had made the fatal mistake of presuming that she could make a successful choir out of Cooney's group of misfits. Some of the girls in the class may well have been able to hold a note or two but with musically challenged boys like Goosey and Pauric on board the project was always doomed. Goosey's singing voice, if one could describe it as such, virtually defied description. No matter what the song, he would literally shout the words out in the same monotonous ear-bleeding tone as if he was attempting to recite a poem that lacked any sort of rhythmic structure. He was so proud of his unfathomably tuneless voice that he would 'sing' ever louder to further massage Breeda's growing temper. Although Pauric was like Charlotte Church in comparison to Goosey, his method of teacher aggravation centred around him changing the words of the songs to whatever came into his head, and he would belt out each note as if he was headlining a gig and had to make do without a microphone.

Following several weeks of getting nowhere with her 'choir', Breeda attempted to reach out to the boys by allowing them to sing something other than old Irish songs and hymns.

The Saw Doctors, an Irish band hailing from Tuam in Co. Galway, had recently burst onto the Irish charts with a song called *I Useta Lover*. The song was so far removed from the normal singing lesson fodder that the boys in the class seemed genuinely enthused as they started into the first verse.

'I have fallen for another she can make her own way home
And even if she asked me now I'd let her go alone
I used to see her up the chapel when she went to Sunday mass
And when she'd go to receive, I'd kneel down there
And watch her pass...'

By now, Pauric was in full flight, and Rams noticed a gleeful look of anticipation flash across his face as he awaited the next line of the song.

'The glory of her ARSE,' bellowed the bold Tighe, placing more emphasis on the last word than on the three preceding it. Of course 'Ass' was the correct lyric and, while that was just about acceptable to Breeda's sensitive ear, 'ARSE' being roared out in the classroom certainly wasn't. It was equivalent to saying 'fuck' instead of its harmless equivalent 'feck'.

Once again it was Pauric's distinctive voice that had betrayed him as the perpetrator of the crime. Breeda dragged him by the ear back into Cooney's class. Teachers have an uncanny ability to make trivial matters sound like world-changing events. Therefore, following Breeda's ample retelling of the events, Cooney was quick to swing into anti-Christ mode.

'500 lines, Tighe,' he yelled.

Such a harsh penalty had previously been reserved for severe acts of terrorism or for when certain boys 'made a show' of the headmaster the time the bishop visited the school. Seemingly use of the word 'arse' fell into the 'terrorism' rather than 'disrespecting religion' category, but the penalty was the same and Pauric was forced to write lines until he was blue in the face.

Given the large amount of stress and annoyance that Cooney had to endure, one might have thought he had little to be happy about. But he must surely have been secretly delighted that his job didn't entail driving the school bus.

Rams and Stano lived about two miles apart and would sit together each morning on the bus. A young farmer, Sean, drove the boys and their fellow students to and from school each day. His job may have looked like a handy number on paper but he faced a plethora of daily distractions as he drove the tin can through miles of potholes, with screaming livestock murdering each other just behind him. Although a mild-mannered man in 'real life', Sean transformed into a mad man of sorts when surrounded by kids who literally ran around the bus as if it was a playground. You couldn't really blame him though. A typical post-school trip on the bus would doubtlessly involve Rams and Stano taking on the majority of the other boys in wrestling matches that would go up and down the aisle. Meanwhile some other children would be putting their half-eaten lunches to good use via large-scale sandwich fights. And, as if things weren't bad enough, every time Gavin O'Dowd disembarked from the bus he would unleash a Hiroshima-type fart, resulting in the few remaining quiet kids stampeding for the windows in search of fresh air.

The noise was deafening and, despite the ongoing commotion, Sean had to get these kids to and from school safely. Most people would surely have quit the job, but he wouldn't throw the towel in without a fight, even if his methods of improving the situation were rather unorthodox.

Sean began carrying a huge stick beside his seat on the bus. As the noise would reach unbearable levels, he'd reach for it and start banging it against the metal roof while roaring like a bear caught in a trap. When the stick waving and roaring failed him, Sean would jam on the breaks, and bodies and bags would fly all over the place. He would then charge down the bus, stick in hand, beating the roof for all its worth. It became an almost daily occurrence, with the kids always looking forward to the bus journey home just to see Sean springing into action for their amusement.

Fortunately for Sean, one in every four weeks, two of his most troublesome passengers granted him a much-needed reprieve. Nevertheless, that didn't guarantee a trouble-free journey.

Rams and Stano had been serving Mass for over a year. There were four teams of altar boys, and each team would serve for a week, beginning on a Sunday morning and finishing the following Saturday evening.

Father Brady was Munterconnaught's parish priest; a genuine, soft-spoken, highly-respected man who took a great interest in the progress of the football team and all things sports-related. His mild-mannered disposition blessed him with the patience of a saint. And, considering the characters who were serving under him, he certainly needed such a quality.

Goosey was Munterconnaught's most diligent altar boy. He went to church every morning and, if—as was often the case—there were a shortage of boys available to serve mass, he'd ensure Father Brady didn't have to run the entire show on his own.

Rams and Stano served on a different team to Goosey, and they cycled to Mass for the pre-school service each time their turn came around. Stano would call by Rams's house on his bike, and the pair would travel the ten-minute journey to the chapel, which was just up a hill past the school. The school bell quickly followed the church service but, once the lessons were over for the day, the lads would hop onto their bikes to head for home – Rams on his trusty BMX and Stano on his shiny black racer. Sean normally drove past the mischievous cyclists shortly before they reached Boylan's crossroads. He always had the foot down hard on the accelerator but never failed to beep the horn for a few seconds while zooming past the lads. Then one evening they decided to treat Sean to a little surprise.

It had been raining almost non-stop for several days, and mud lined both sides of the road. With Boylan's almost in sight, the mischievous pair pulled up on the road. Stano flung his bike into a hedge, and picked up the biggest pile of mud he could carry in his two hands. Rams quickly followed suit, and the two waited for the bus to approach. They weren't kept waiting. Within seconds, Sean and the big fun bus came thundering around the corner and—bang—mud bombs plastered the windscreen, turning it into a devastating brown mess with a few tiny spots of glass barely visible. Sean hit the brakes harder than usual as Rams and Stano stood by the road laughing their arses off. Having only devised this most heinous of crimes just moments before putting it into action, the lads seemed to think that Sean would see the funny side of it. But as he sprang out of the bus like a demented Jack in the Box and began running towards the little terrors, they quickly realised that this was not the case.

Stano was standing closer to the bus than the Rams, so he was obviously the fuming driver's initial target. But Stano was also faster and more agile than his mate and, as he quickly vaulted the nearby hedge, he could hear Sean roaring behind him.

'Come back here, ya little fucker.'

By the time Sean turned round to look for the Rams, the delinquent was in an adjoining field to Stano, running as if his very life depended on it. It took some serious grovelling and apologising the following Monday morning before Rams and Stano could travel on the bus again and, despite the unprovoked nature of the attack, Sean didn't report the incident to their parents or Cooney, thus saving the lads from what surely would have been a severe punishment.

One might imagine that the one person who would have been free of the hardship endured by Cooney and Sean would have been Father Brady. But his job also proved difficult on occasion.

Although serving Mass wasn't exactly on a par with sky diving in terms of excitement, the silence that was synonymous with the job often served to inspire the lads to create devilment rather than spend time praying. Seniority dictated which of the altar boys delegated the various 'jobs'. These ranged from presenting the water and wine to the priest, to holding the plate under the chins of each member of the congregation. The plate job was particularly empowering as it allowed one the opportunity to 'get one over' on school friends by holding the plate firmly against an individual's neck while smirking at him, safe in the knowledge that he could do nothing about it in the safe confines of the church.

But by far the greatest honour that could be bestowed upon an altar boy was the job of 'ringing the bell'. The bell was of the old-fashioned, heavy-duty gong variety, and the accompanying weighty handle allowed the holder to think that he was brandishing a lump hammer. Therefore, the unspoken challenge at each sermon entailed the chosen altar boy driving the lump hammer into the bell with as much force as he could get away with. It was no surprise when the top of the handle eventually became loose after months of abuse. But a quick clockwise turn seemed to fix the problem.

One day Stano, giddy with excitement after being assigned bell duty, forgot to tighten the top of the troublesome handle during the sermon. He looked rather pleased with himself as he struck the bell like a bongo drum, each ring resonating ever louder throughout the church. As Father Brady lifted the chalice above his head, Stano clobbered the bell for the final time. This time the top of the handle whizzed through the air, hitting the unsuspecting priest with a thump on his left ankle. Fortunately, Father Brady wasn't one for hysterics. So he continued the sermon and afterwards gently reminded Stano that the bell needed, 'only a light touch'.

While Stano had no illusions of perfection when it came to serving Mass, Rams wrongly considered himself to be a consummate professional. But he proved to be more than capable of causing unnecessary, albeit unintentional stress for Father Brady.

It was Easter and, prior to the start of the Sunday sermon, Father Brady asked Rams to light a few of the small candles, which were arranged on a circular stand about twenty feet from the altar. Common sense dictated that one should begin by lighting the candles at the far end of the stand and then working towards the nearest ones, but the Rams was never one for convention.

Lighting the candles nearest to him, he then proceeded to light the ones furthest away from him and in doing so the left sleeve of his altar gown caught fire. As he returned to the sacristy, oblivious that his entire arm was in flames, he was somewhat surprised to turn around and discover Father Brady frantically hitting his arm in an attempt to smother the flames.

As the priest lamented the loss of one of only a handful of altar gowns, a small smile appeared on Rams's face as he slowly realised that he had set himself on fire at Mass in front of a packed house, and he hadn't even meant to do it. Not even Stano could top that.

Chapter 4

PRANKS AND PETS

SEPTEMBER 1990 signified the beginning of the end of Rams's primary school education as he entered Sixth Class. As ever, the lads were up to their old tricks and, by the second day back at school, Goosey had devised his latest prank.

The rubbish bin, which served the entire class, was located beside the door leading to the toilets and staff room. It was nothing more than a cardboard box over which the kids sharpened their pencils and where the more troublesome amongst them were forced to stand each time Cooney ordered them to 'go to the corner' for some or other misdemeanour.

With Cooney in the staff room, Goosey set to work. He moved the bin closer to the doorway so that the back of the door would, when opened, make contact with the springy sides of the box. Then, under his orders, the class erupted with enough noise as to almost bring the ceiling tumbling down.

Cooney came thundering through the door, sending it swinging towards the box. As envisaged by the crafty Goosey, the door rebounded off the box and returned like a boomerang to the headmaster, hitting him square on the forehead with such force that one could almost see stars circling his wounded cranium. In a bid to save face, he only briefly felt the lump that was already rising just above his nose, and he then marched towards the door at the opposite end of the room, which led to Breeda's class. It was several minutes later before he returned, red faced and unable to find a culprit for his 'accident'.

Just over a week later it was Goosey's twelfth birthday, which was accompanied by an obligatory party. Rams and Stano walked to the birthday boy's house after school, eager to get the dinner out of the way so that they could concentrate on stuffing their faces with the multitude of cakes and buns that Goosey's mother had provided. With the formal part of the evening over, the three lads went outside to play football and, after almost putting the ball through the kitchen window, Goosey decided that a game of Hide-and-Seek was in order.

It turned out that Goosey's pet dog, Rambo, was a male collie with more than a few tricks up his fur-lined sleeve. As instructed by Goosey, each of the lads in turn let Rambo sniff them, thereby picking up their scent. With Goosey holding Rambo tightly by the collar, the two lads hid amongst the trees and shrubbery in the large back garden. Once they were safely in place, Goosey released Rambo, and the smart collie accurately traced the lads' footsteps until finding them.

Seeing how Rambo operated, Rams and Stano decided to try to make things a bit more difficult for the collie. Therefore, in the course of hiding, they placed a trail of objects in Rambo's path, all conveniently sourced from the garage. A lawnmower, ladder and broken down washing machine were all placed in the path of the soon to be released pet, but in true Geraghty fashion, Rambo wasn't to be denied and therefore managed to vault all of the obstacles, capturing each of the boys as before. Stano claimed that his dog, Blackie, was even smarter but it would be a few months later before the full extent of Blackie's 'talents' would be revealed.

Just six weeks later saw the arrival of Halloween, which brought with it a chance for the lads to dress up in a bid to receive generous helpings of sweets from their neighbours. 'Trick or Treating'—a tradition originating in Ireland—was extremely popular in the country, and had for years been a favourite with each of the boys. Knowing that in less than a year from now they would be attending secondary school, hence leaving this primary school activity behind them, the three lads were really looking forward to hounding the residents of Munterconnaught for chocolates one last time.

The evening started quite well and, with their carrier bags bulging with all sorts of delicious goodies, the boys eventually reached the last house on their journey. It was home to an old spinster, Miss Shaw, about whom the lads knew little other than the local rumour that she resembled a witch and had a personality to match her unfortunate appearance. After several persistent knocks by the Rams on the front door, a porch light suddenly came alive and the spinster appeared as if from nowhere.

'Trick or treat,' roared the boys, their faces hidden by cheap plastic masks.

Although the Rams had initially voiced concerns about visiting the witch's house, his feelings of unease quickly subsided when the smiling and seemingly normal woman reached for a big tin of *Cadbury Roses*, and proceeded to give generous helpings of Rams's favourite chocolates to him and each of his friends. The lads, delighted with their good luck, bid her a fond farewell. They were barely out the front gate when Goosey, ever the hungry bastard, quickly ripped the wrapper off one of the chocolates, and popped it into his mouth. Had it not been pitch dark, he might have spotted that the sweets were a bit suspect, and he would surely have opted to go hungry instead.

A sharp roar of pain emanated from his mouth, followed by a spit, and then some choice expletives.

'What the fuck? The bitch gave us a heap of stones.'

True enough, all of the roses had been taken out of their wrappers and meticulously replaced with stones, the rest of which could have caused even more damage than the one that left Goosey with a cracked tooth.

The lads were fuming but, after a brief debate, decided against retaliation of any sort. But it was somewhat ironic that, following years of playing tricks on others, it was Goosey who had been Miss Shaw's main victim on that Halloween night. Nonetheless, he remained unperturbed and, if anything, seemed inspired by the joke that had been played on him. Therefore, just a few weeks later he attempted one of his most disgusting pranks yet.

It was an unusually mild November day, and the three lads were playing soccer in the schoolyard. The Rams stood in goals as per usual, simultaneously playing the part of referee while Goosey and Stano squared off against each other in a thrilling contest. Two large pillars—which partly supported a rain shelter and were located at the side of the old school—served adequately as goalposts. The old school gable wall, which was perpendicular to the shelter, provided valuable assistance in scoring the most bizarre goals, thanks to its close proximity to the goals. It wasn't exactly a Croke Park set-up, but it was a venue where the lads enjoyed many a memorable game of football.

This had been a particularly hard-fought contest and, as Goosey excused himself for a short timeout, he brought with him the can of orange he had been supping on over the course of the match. Upon his return a few moments later, he was quick to offer the Rams a drink but, since he had been standing in goal, he wasn't particularly thirsty and declined the offer. Stano, on the other hand, was dying for a drink. Grabbing the can, he took a big mouthful, swallowing so quickly that his taste buds barely had time to get to work.

'That's fierce warm orange, Goosey,' he gasped.

Goosey began convulsing in laughter, and slowly it began dawning on Stano that his friend had been taking the piss, and quite literally at that. He put his nose to the can, confirming his worst fears. It seemed that nobody was safe from Goosey and his bag of tricks.

A few weeks later, and with that particularly revolting trick forgotten, Stano would finally have the chance to prove to Goosey that his pet dog was capable of leaving Rambo in the shade when it came to performing tricks and impressing all around him.

It was Stano's thirteenth birthday party and, like Goosey's hooley a few months earlier, the family pet was getting more attention than usual. Blackie was a cute little terrier that was, as the name implies, as black as the night. After the birthday formalities, the three lads went out to Stano's back garden where, in an effort to impress the lads, he tried to get Blackie to perform some of the tricks that he had spent the previous few weeks teaching him. But Blackie wasn't having any of it, and Stano, quickly losing patience with the terrier, suggested to the lads that they get away from the house by walking up the lane, which was located beside and beyond the grounds of his home.

In rural Ireland, going for a walk or cycle in a bid to explore the countryside and escape the watchful eyes of one's parents was always the perfect alternative to the never-ending games of football that were played every day up and down the country. The Rams loved the one-mile walk up the lane. Maybe it was the old railway tracks and abandoned carriages that captured his imagination, or perhaps it was the ever-present peace and tranquillity while catching tadpoles in the small stream that made it such a joyful experience.

Blackie diligently followed the lads up the lane despite his scolding from Stano moments earlier. They were just passing the river when Stano realised that he was, to put it lightly, 'dying for a shite'. At this stage, he knew that heading for home was not an option. So, asking the two lads to look in the other direction, he loosened his trousers and then his bowels, graciously leaving a colossal dump beside the river. Feeling very much relieved and a stone lighter, he walked back to where his friends were waiting.

'What's Blackie doing?' asked the Rams.

Stano looked over and couldn't believe what he was witnessing. Blackie, perhaps in an attempt to make amends for not performing any tricks earlier in the hour, was wolfing down Stano's shite. It was almost as if the dog hadn't been fed in a fortnight and, now all of a sudden, had being presented with a 20-ounce fillet steak.

'Get away from it, Blackie,' begged Stano as he gently tried using his foot to move the dog away from the meal.

Consumed by hunger, Blackie feigned deafness and, as the lads looked on in equal measures of delight and horror, the faithful pet did his master proud in a way Rambo could never manage: by eating in its entirety the unsightly mess left on the lane by Stano.

And they say you can't teach an old dog new tricks.

Chapter 5

WRESTLING WITH CIDER

TWO MONTHS after Stano's birthday, the Rams reached his thirteenth year. Although his personality was far from being completely developed, he was already exhibiting many of the same traits, morals and habits as both of his parents.

His mother, Nuala, was the loud, larger-than-life personality of the household, whose voice—like that of the Rams—was probably audible from outer space. She had somewhat of a mad streak in her, and her vocabulary perfectly complimented her infectious personality. Every few words uttered from her mouth seemed to give mention to 'Fuck' or 'Jaysis' and yet, when the Rams would casually drop such words into everyday household conversation, she would inevitably think that the influence of his friends was to blame for his poor behaviour.

'That's Derek Stanley's dirty talk,' she would say to him, and then seconds later she would be heard roaring, 'Jaysis Christ, the dinner's fucking ruined', while opening the oven door to an over-cooked meal. Unsurprisingly, she went down a treat with any visiting children and, many years later, Gooscy would take much delight in performing exaggerated impersonations.

'Fuck, fuck, fuck. Ya little bollocks. Pass me the fucking salt. Fuck, fuck, fuck,' he would typically go, and the Rams would laugh heartily at this over the top interpretation.

Despite the hard exterior, Nuala had a heart of gold and, although often strict with her children, it was never without reason and their best interests at heart. She brought them up to realise that, 'Money isn't everything', 'Your health is your wealth', and 'Good manners go a long way'. Unlike many other parents, she never assumed that her children were angels, and rather than saying, 'My child wouldn't do that', when confronted by an irate parent or teacher, she would take the accused child aside and ask them to tell her the truth regarding the situation. She would then deal with the matter as required, and the subject would be dropped thereafter.

Nuala also taught her children to stand up for themselves and that nobody, no matter what their wealth or position, was in any way better than they were. That particular lesson would make a significant impression on the Rams and how he would develop as a man over the following years.

Rams's father, Jimmy, also served as a worthy role model. He was a quiet, unassuming man, well liked by all who knew him and the personification of what a gentleman should be. He worked hard his whole life—often six days a week—as a builder and later as a maintenance man but, being a victim of the recession-hit eighties, he never reaped the financial rewards for which his talents—expert brick laying, tiling and painting amongst them—truly deserved. He rarely drank, enjoyed the simpler things in life and loved fishing, playing pool and watching wrestling.

It was from about this time that the Rams also began to take an interest in the weird and largely misunderstood world of professional wrestling. It started with a trip to Kells to see Giant Haystacks competing against some unknown grappler. Haystacks was a giant of a man who weighed in at about 50 stone, and is best remembered throughout Ireland and Britain for his infamous matches with the equally generously-boned Big Daddy.

Unfortunately for the Rams, on this particular occasion Haystacks's much-hyped appearance in the historic Meath town wasn't to be. Despite the frequent assurances of the ring announcer, Haystacks did not arrive in the field by helicopter as planned. Nonetheless, the Rams enjoyed the remaining matches for which he had a ringside view.

Following this disappointment, Rams began tuning in weekly to UTV to watch NWA Wrestling, which shortly thereafter would become World Championship Wrestling (WCW). Wrestlers with names like Sting, 'Nature Boy' Ric Flair, Sid Vicious and the world's tallest athlete, El Gigante, would never fail to liven up a Saturday afternoon. Rams's father would also stop whatever he was doing so that he could sit down in front of the television to watch the show. He would then cheer on his favourite wrestlers for the next hour, shouting the odds every time a bad guy got away with some or other transgression behind the referee's back. Much to the amusement of Rams's two sisters, Nuala eventually caught the wrestling bug too, and the girls were left wondering if their parents had finally lost the plot.

The 'Wrestling Three' would take things further a few years later following the relegation of their favourite show from a Saturday afternoon slot to 2.30 am on a Thursday night. Undeterred by the knowledge that Jimmy would be working the next day and the Rams would have school, all three of them would set their watches for 2.20 am, which would allow them just enough time to make some crisp sandwiches and grab a comfortable spot in the sitting room for the main event of the night. As he grew older, the Rams would look fondly back on those times while admitting that such late night bonding wasn't exactly typical of the average family. But then again, the Smith family was anything but average and, as the Rams's last ever day of primary school approached, Cooney should have suspected that such a significant day would be far from average.

As was often the case, Goosey played a big part in ensuring that the occasion didn't go smoothly. The ironic thing was that earlier in the day Cooney presented Goosey with a trophy for missing only one day's schooling in six years. With such a glowing record, surely Goosey would be the last person to cast a shadow over the remainder of the day?

It was lunchtime and spilling rain outside, forcing the lads to stay indoors playing Blind Man's Buff. The boys' toilets were always the popular venue of choice for this particular game, mainly because the cloakroom was part of the same room, which—combined with the urinals, sink area and various other nooks and crannies—provided a room with a surprisingly large amount of hiding places.

The disadvantage of this unusual set-up was undoubtedly the smell. At least once a day somebody was likely to leave a large deposit in the toilet, which wouldn't have been too bad had the offender seen fit to flush afterwards. Word would quickly circulate around the class that there was something worth seeing in the toilet, and then each of the lads would ask Cooney for permission to use the facilities. Upon returning, they would confirm to their nearest mate that the 'brown monster' had indeed landed. Although it doesn't paint the prettiest of pictures, this carry-on provided plenty of entertainment for the boys during classes.

The toilets also provided a platform for all manner of grotesque thrills when playing Blind Man's Buff, and it was no different on the final day of school. Pauric Tighe was playing the part of the blind man, walking around with a coat on his head while trying to navigate the darkness. Rams was hiding beside the urinal. Two others were barely moving behind a few coats that were hanging up, and Stano was hovering precariously over the toilet bowl with his hand covering his nose in a futile attempt to block the unbearable smell from invading his nostrils.

Two benches ran parallel to each other along each side of the cloakroom and, while a game of Blind Man's Buff was in progress, it was common practice to move one of the benches so that it partially blocked the door, thereby keeping unwanted visits from the headmaster to a minimum.

All of a sudden, there came a pounding on the door. Presuming it to be Cooney, each of the lads abandoned their hiding places and grabbed a place on the bench that wasn't holding the door and the would-be visitor at bay. While attempting to abandon his hiding place, Stano slipped and was still cursing his urine-soaked foot when the Rams opened the door to reveal none other than Goosey.

He was carrying a plastic carrier bag and, delving inside, surprised everyone by producing a can of cider. As the lads became carried away in celebrating what a rebel Goosey was for stealing the alcohol from his parents' drinks cabinet, nobody seemed to notice that, as the can was passed from one set of hands to the next, it was being shaken and dropped repeatedly so that it was almost fit to explode.

Therefore, when Goosey opened the can to toast the lads and their last day of school, cider flew ferociously from the top of the can, spraying the wall and forming a sizable puddle on the piss-stained floor. The resulting commotion attracted the attention of Cooney who, in the absence of the bench acting as a barrier, rushed into the cloak-room wanting to know what the source of all the noise was.

Spotting the empty container on the floor, he flew into a rage and demanded to know who had disgraced themselves by bringing alcohol into school. Nobody spoke, forcing Cooney to cancel the end-of-year party, which was due to take place later that afternoon in the old school.

Back in the classroom, close to an hour of unbearable silence had passed. With the time for the party drawing ever closer, Pauric Tighe stood up and cleared his throat.

Cooney wouldn't have been at all surprised if a confession from Tighe was on the cards. His disciplinary record was comparable to that of a death row inmate. But, like the three lads in the class above him, he was a resourceful little bastard when he needed to be, and he had no intention of hanging a noose round his own neck.

'Sir, I think it might have been Jacob who brought in the alcohol.'

'Was it you, Jacob?' bellowed Cooney.

Jacob was a shy, quiet boy, who wouldn't have dreamed of commit-ting such a crime, but he was also incapable of speaking clearly. As he began mumbling his defence, his cheeks flushed red as if an admission of guilt. Unable to understand Jacob, and with no patience remaining, Cooney was quick to deal with the guilty-as-charged villain.

'1,000 lines, Jacob.'

Incensed by the incident and prolonged silence in the aftermath of said incident, and with Jacob not denying the charge, Cooney set a new record in punishment that would keep the poor lad writing until the ink ran dry in his biro.

As Jacob began his laborious exercise, the lads breathed a collective sigh of relief while stuffing their faces at the on-again party.

Rams, Goosey and Stano had enjoyed some great times over the years and were now ready to bring the wisecracking, pranks and laughter to a new level: secondary school.

But was secondary school ready for them?

Chapter 6

THE PAINMASTER

D ESPITE LIVING in a small, remote parish in rural Ireland, the residents of Munterconnaught had several options available to them when the time came to seek further education for their children after they finished primary school.

For many parents, the most obvious choice was between the post-primary schools in Oldcastle and Virginia. Munterconnaught was located roughly halfway—eight kilometres—between the two small towns, but school buses only served St Olivers in Oldcastle, making it the logical choice for many. From the by now 12 students in Rams's primary school class, four opted for secondary school education in Oldcastle, four for Virginia and the remainder elsewhere, including the nearby town of Kells.

Much to their delight, Rams, Goosey and Stano found themselves attending school together in Oldcastle. With eight years of a solid friendship behind them, they swore they would always remain close friends despite all the new people they would surely meet at St Olivers.

Therefore, it was perhaps surprising that almost immediately after classes commenced in September, the lads began to hang out in different groups instead of forming friendships within the same circle of people. All three of them were placed in separate classes upon joining first year, only sharing some same sex classes such as P.E. and Woodwork. In fact Rams and Goosey wouldn't attend any of the same classes for the first few years at St Olivers, meaning that they usually only got a chance to catch up on the bus on the way to and from school each day.

The school bus was one of three serving Munterconnaught and the adjoining parishes. Rams and Goosey travelled on the same bus, where Rams found it to be very different to the stick-waving days of Sean. The driver of the secondary school bus was a no-nonsense, no-personality tyrant who didn't have a problem putting someone off the bus for the slightest offence. As such, the students had to keep the noise down or face the consequences.

Back at school, the Rams had befriended Donny Farrelly who sat beside him for some classes. Donny was a jovial decent guy but, as the days and weeks passed by, Rams realised that he and Donny were very different people and didn't really have that much in common. Without wanting to offend him, the Rams didn't quite know how he might give him the brush off, and that's where Sean George Mara II came into the picture.

Most people knew him by his surname, Mara, but the Rams like to occasionally call him Sean George Mara II 'for short'. George was his middle name and the Rams reckoned that the II added to the end of his name just seemed right. As time went by at St Olivers, the Rams became responsible for 'christening' several other students. The case of Stephen Farrelly was a typical example.

One day, from out of nowhere, the Rams began referring to Stephen as 'Fingering Joe'. Most people would agree that it wasn't the most flattering alias and, before long, the 'Fingering' part of the name disappeared, and Stephen became known to almost all who knew him as just 'Joe'. Joe seemed to like his new identity even though the Rams had just plucked the name out of his ass during a moment of boredom.

Mark Tuite was another individual whose alter ego the Rams played a part in creating. Like the Rams, Mark was an avid wrestling fan in the early nineties. In 1992, a wrestler by the name of Ron Simmons became the first African American to win world championship heavyweight gold. Simmons, due to his previously successful career in American football, was known as the 'All-American'. Mark began referring to himself as the 'All-Irishman', and henceforth, the Rams referred to Mark as 'Big Ron'. In no time, everyone came to know the All-Irishman as 'Ron' and, to this day, many people are oblivious to his real identity.

Ron lived in Boolies, an area just outside Oldcastle. Having attended primary school in the town with Sean George Mara II amongst others, he was accustomed to Mara's unique personality.

The Rams, on the other hand, initially didn't know what to make of Mara. He first clapped eyes on him in French class during the introductory week of school. The Rams was sitting quietly in a corner of the classroom awaiting the arrival of the teacher when Mara approached and asked if he could sit in the vacant seat next to him. Within a few days and, following numerous conversations between the pair, Mara invited the Rams to his house in Oldcastle to shoot some pool at the weekend. But Rams gently declined the offer since he didn't really fancy cycling eight kilometres to play pool with someone he barely knew.

After a few weeks the Rams attempted to appease Mara by inviting him to join himself and Donny for a game of pool at lunchtime in the Ceili House bar. Mara accepted the offer and joined the pair in the bar that afternoon.

Donny and Mara knew each other from primary school and, therefore, were very familiar with each other. Mara seemed to take great delight in winding Donny up by distracting him each time he'd attempt to take a shot at the pool table. Donny had a bit of a short fuse and couldn't handle the daily harassments so, following two weeks of constant goading, he walked out the door of the Ceili House and didn't return.

Mara and Rams continued to play pool together everyday during lunchtime, and eventually Stano joined the elite group. As the days went by, the Rams came to realise that he had more in common with Mara that he had originally thought.

Although Rams was very laid back and easy going, Mara took things to a different level. He didn't seem to give a shit about anything in so far as he didn't take anything too seriously and one would almost have to take out a gun and shoot him just to bring him close to losing his temper. To him, there was no point in ever getting stressed out over trivial matters, and this carefree attitude made him a person whom one couldn't but like.

Mara was also a wrestling fan and, within weeks of meeting, he and the Rams were unofficially operating as a tag team around the schoolyard. Mara was stocky and as strong as an ox, and the Rams was as skinny as a rake, which meant he could fly through the air, landing on the broken bodies that would be assembled on the ground by Sean George.

Mara's move of choice was the 'powerbomb', which involved placing his victim's head between his legs, lifting him off the ground by his waist, and then slamming him onto the ground so that he would land heavily on his back. Fortunately, Mara hadn't quite perfected the move meaning that his unwilling opponents often managed to escape just prior to being slammed, thereby avoiding injury.

Mara had 'borrowed' this move from one of his favourite wrestlers, Big Van Vader, who was also referred to on television as 'The man they call Vader'. Rams began calling himself, 'The man they call the Rams', and borrowed liberally from Vader's phrasebook when he would tell people, 'I feel no pain, I fear no man.'

Rams wasn't totally bullshitting because, as it happened, he had a relatively high pain threshold. Even if he did injure himself in a skirmish, he would pretend that he was fine, and would laugh off his injuries, much to the bemusement of those around him.

At this time, many of the Rams's main classes were held in prefabs at the back of the school. Most students hung out in the assembly hall for the duration of the 11 o'clock break and, following the school bell sounding, the quickest way back to the prefabs involved passing through an adjoining corridor, which was known to the First Year boys as 'the gauntlet'.

The gauntlet was where all of the senior boys congregated during the daily break. They would form a line on each side of the narrow hallway, waiting for fresh prey. As soon as any brave or foolish First

Year boys stepped into the trap, they would suffer a severe beating from one end of the corridor to the other.

Most of the First Year boys were scared shitless when faced with the gauntlet and, rather than risk a relentless beating, would choose to take a long roundabout walk to get back to the prefabs.

Not so Mara and the Rams. Every day the two would run at the gauntlet. Punches and kicks would seemingly bounce off Mara's large frame as he fought his way through, whereas Rams's smaller size and greater speed meant that he was more difficult to hit. Although he would still take quite a pounding, he would brush himself off upon reaching the end of the gauntlet, turn around, and wish his antagonists, 'Better luck next time.'

On one occasion, Rams and Mara managed to reach the safety of the prefabs completely unscathed. The two boys were in different classes until later that afternoon, and only a small cloakroom separated the two rooms. Mara took a seat for his upcoming English lesson, and the Rams did likewise in the opposite classroom. While awaiting the arrival of the teacher, he looked out the window only to see two of his most dangerous adversaries staring in at him: David Hanlon and Ollie Briody. These two behemoths were amongst the toughest boys in the school.

Hanlon, the bulkier of the two, was incredibly strong. It was rumoured that one night as he was leaving a disco in Athboy, eight teens followed him down the street and attacked him. Hanlon grabbed the ringleader, knocked him to the ground and sat on him. For every box Hanlon received from the others, his victim received two devastating blows to the head. To prevent their friend from suffering permanent injuries, the aggressors were forced to retreat from the scene, leaving Hanlon to his own devices. Therefore, the story goes that eight men alone cannot take Hanlon down; maybe nine might fare better.

Ollie Briody was no pushover either. He was one of the tallest boys in the school, two years ahead of the Rams, and built like a tank. Supposedly there's safety in numbers so one day at lunchtime when Rams, Stano and Mara spotted Ollie standing alone on a hill at the side of the sports pitch, they seized the opportunity. Mara hit Ollie

from behind with a powerful shoulder block and that, coupled with
the contributed gravitational pull from the hill, sent the giant falling
to the ground. The boys could barely believe their luck, and didn't
waste any time capitalising on their good fortune. All three jumped
on Ollie's back and began punching him. Stano and Mara must have
sensed that the giant was stirring because no sooner were they on his
back than they were off it again, running for their lives. Meanwhile
the Rams was too occupied putting Ollie into his patented sleeper
hold to notice that his friends were not behind him helping to keep the
big man pinned down.

All of a sudden, in a scene somewhat reminiscent of *Gulliver's
Travels*, the giant rose from the ground, with the Lilliputian hanging
from his neck. Grabbing the Rams's arms, he swung him around for
several seconds before launching him like a Frisbee over the hill from
whence he came.

In truth, there was never any bad blood between the Rams and the
two giants. In fact he enjoyed the friendly battles most of the time but,
when staring out the prefab window that spring afternoon, he knew he
was in a wee bit of trouble.

Hanlon and Ollie were out for blood due to Rams's triumphant and
cocky run through the gauntlet moments earlier. They barged into the
packed classroom screaming blue murder, but the Rams managed to
sidestep them and made a beeline for Mara's classroom in an attempt
to get reinforcements. With no time to waste, he gave the door a mer-
ciful kick, sending it flying open.

'Mara, give me a hand. They're out to fucking kill me,' he roared at
the top of his voice.

Rams's jaw dropped as he faced a silenced room and a very pissed
off English teacher, Martin O'Reilly, who had just seconds earlier
commenced his class. For once, words failed the Rams so he quickly
closed the door, ran back to his class and took his seat in the hope that
O'Reilly had a very short memory. Hanlon and Ollie had wisely scam-
pered, but now Rams was in a different kind of trouble. Fortunately,
he escaped with just a bollocking and so lived to fight another day.

Unsurprisingly, Hanlon and Ollie weren't the only senior students who would have enjoyed taking the Rams down a peg or two. Ronan Crawley was one such person. He was in Third Year and was also amongst the toughest boys in the school. Crawley liked issuing 'dead legs' to anyone who pissed him off and, having received one on more than a few occasions, the Rams knew that Crawley's dead legs were amongst the most painful going.

It was about halfway through the 11 o'clock break, and the Rams stood in the packed assembly hall talking to a few girls from his year. Crawley, thinking he would show Rams up in front of them, approached him and, without warning, delivered a most devastating dead leg that would have left any other First Year boy lying on the floor clutching his leg. The assembly hall fell quiet as the students awaited a scream of agony from the Rams. But it was not forthcoming. Although he had felt the full force of Crawley's attack, he would not allow his leg to buckle and, with a wry smile spreading across his face, he turned to face him.

'I hope you didn't hurt yourself, son.'

Crawley was gob smacked. He had no reply and, as the nearby students laughed their arses off, he quietly slipped out of the hall, scratching his head while wondering what exactly had just taken place. Maybe it was true; maybe the Rams really did feel no pain.

Chapter 7

RAYMOND, RONAN AND RED CARDS

IN HIS eight years spent at Knocktemple National School, the Rams had been educated by, and had in turn tormented, just three teachers. His arrival at St Olivers brought with it opportunities aplenty to harass significantly more of them, and he was only too willing to oblige.

By the time Rams had commenced Second Year at the school, he had all of the teachers sussed. He knew which of them wouldn't tolerate any of his messing but, as luck would have it, those particular individuals were in the minority. Therefore, the Rams learnt to 'play' each teacher differently.

Science was one of his favourite subjects, not because of the subject matter but because the inmates were undoubtedly running the asylum during this class.

For Science classes, the Rams sat beside Terry Kiernan, or Tezzer as some people called him. As was typical of the Rams, he would sometimes 'shorten' Terry's name to 'Terence Trent D'Arby' after the famous eighties chart topper. Terry was one of the most down-to-earth blokes the Rams had ever met. He had a wicked sense of humour and always seemed to be laughing and joking but, unlike the Rams, he seldom over-stepped the mark in class, thereby usually managing to stay clear of trouble.

The boys and girls attended separate Science classes, with Paddy Traynor having the unenviable task of teaching over 20 of the boys, each of them louder and bolder than the next. Unbeknownst to him, Traynor was nicknamed Paddy Apparatus, mainly because his job regularly entailed him saying, 'Set up the apparatus.'

It was a harmless nickname but definitely one befitting a science teacher. Unfortunately for Paddy, his soft nature meant that his students' behaviour often bordered on criminal because they knew that following their latest act of debauchery Paddy would most likely just shout the odds for a bit and that's the worst that would happen. Then after maybe 30 seconds of silence from the students, they would continue where they left off and the noise would reach near deafening levels as the vicious cycle looped endlessly.

The Rams chose to lead by example when it came to antagonising poor Paddy. He would act like there was no teacher in the room by carrying on conversations with some of the boys at the other side of the Science lab. Meanwhile Paddy would try his best to continue teaching the class, but he would eventually lose his temper and begin the speech that the Rams quickly grew to love due to its unintentional humour.

Being a teacher, Paddy was one of the few people—apart from Rams's family members—who called him by his Christian name, but he could never seem to remember whether Rams's real name was Ronan or, for some reason, Raymond. Rather than opting for one or other of the names, he would always choose both.

'Good God almighty; Raymond or Ronan. By God, I have kids at home and they're only five or six and, by Jesus, they have more sense than ya.'

The fact that Paddy also seemed to be unsure as to how old his own children were didn't help the Rams to keep a straight face in front of a visibly agitated teacher. On one occasion, following more smart-assed remarks than usual by his daily tormentor, Paddy made the mistake of saying, 'Raymond or Ronan, do you think I'm stupid?'

Most students would have kept quiet and allowed Paddy to vent his understandable frustration, but this comment was like a red rag to the Rams.

'Well, do you really want me to answer that?'

Somehow the Rams was allowed to stay in the class after that most audacious reply, meaning that he, along with the rest of the lads, could continue making Paddy's life hell by shouting, breaking thermometers and setting each other alight at every given opportunity.

One teacher who certainly wasn't about to put up with the Rams's delinquent-like behaviour was Mrs. Colgan, the Physical Education teacher. P.E. classes at St Olivers consisted of a limited selection of sports: basketball, soccer, badminton, gymnastics, hockey and rounders (a form of baseball).

The Rams didn't much care for basketball, but occasionally enjoyed the weekly games if Stano was on the opposing team. Stano was better at sports than most but, like the Rams, basketball wouldn't have been a particular favourite of his. Both he and the Rams were more accustomed to the rough and tumble of Gaelic football than a sport where physical contact was all but impossible. But that didn't deter the two from charging into each other and tackling hard at every given opportunity. If a decision went against Stano, he was always likely to drop kick the basketball to the far end of the court, resulting in his instant dismissal from the game. A red card for the Rams often followed for his post-card jeering at Stano who would be standing at the sidelines fuming over Colgan's 'unfair decision' moments earlier.

Gymnastics was another sport that both of the boys detested yet ironically enjoyed at the same time. The gym mats on the hall floor provided the perfect place for the Rams to put his infamous 'wrestling skills' to the test. With Colgan's back turned, he would perform dropkicks into thin air, landing on the mat in a heap while simultaneously letting out an almighty roar.

The commotion would continue each time the class was required to perform the 'handstand' manoeuvre. As soon as the Rams was completely balanced on his head, he would begin shouting at the top of his voice until losing his balance and crashing to the mat, slamming his feet as hard as he could while roaring as if he'd been dropped from a 50-storey building. Understandably, Colgan would flip the lid, only calming down after the Rams would explain that the blood going to his head had caused this inexplicable and uncontrollable Tourette-like condition. The Rams had an uncanny ability to talk his way out of almost any ridiculous self-created situation and he seemed to thrive on pushing Colgan as far as he could.

Soccer was one of the few sports Rams truly enjoyed playing. Whenever it was part of the P.E. curriculum he'd play in goal and occasionally venture up front when it took his fancy. Although seldom sent off during a game, the Rams held the unprecedented distinction of being red-carded on two separate occasions before the beginning of a match.

The first time was as a result of sarcastically offering to do an extra warm-up lap of the field prior to a match, and then refusing to do so when Colgan accepted his offer. The second such dismissal occurred when the Rams happened upon a garden rake that the janitor had accidentally left behind on the football field. Picking it up, he proceeded to run around, balancing the rake on one finger while roaring as if he had been shot. When Colgan arrived on the field, the Rams knew that his time on the same pitch was up, and so it was that he received his second pre-match sending off. Not even the controversial Roy Keane could have equalled that record.

Although St Olivers was a significantly larger school than Knocktemple, the Rams was pleased that the change in setting proved to be inconsequential in many respects. Goosey and Stano were still occasionally causing mischief by his side, most teachers were helpless victims of his limitless one-liners, and P.E. was almost as much fun as it had been during the glory days of the 'McGovern era'. A prize for whoever said, 'School days are the best days of your life.'

Chapter 8

IT DOESN'T ALWAYS RAIN IN MAYO

APRIL 1993 brought with it the opportunity for the Rams to go on a three-day school tour to Mayo. He had been on many one-day tours over the years, ranging from primary school trips, which usually incorporated a visit to Kells and Dublin Zoo, to the Munterconnaught Pioneer club excursions, which annually took in exotic locations such as Bray and Salthill.

The Rams always anticipated a visit to Dublin with much enthusiasm because the hustle and bustle of the capital was a far cry from the quiet country life he was accustomed to in Cavan. Part of a Sixth Class tour saw Rams and his classmates visiting the Natural History Museum of Ireland. Glass closures surrounded only some of the exhibits. Therefore, Rams found himself face to face with a giant bear during the course of a guided tour of the museum. The beast stood over six feet tall and, although dead for many years, still looked like it would tear the face of anyone who dared come too close.

Being the inquisitive little tearaway that he was, the Rams just had to know what the last meal consumed by the ferocious animal had been. Finding a stool nearby and, with nobody looking in his direction, he hopped onto it, stared the bear in the mouth and shoved his left arm as far down the throat of the unsuspecting carcass as he could manage. The handful of straw-like material he recovered confirmed his suspicions, and he threw his find to the ground in disappointment as the tour guide approached. Fortunately, the

Munterconnaught tour bus arrived back in Cavan before the guide discovered that somebody had been interfering with the bear. But a stern letter some days later from the museum to Cooney ensured that the class wouldn't be revisiting the capital any time soon.

Fast forward to 1993 and the Rams was ready for his big trip to Mayo. Financial constraints over the years meant that family holidays had never been an option in the Smith household. Discounting a few short stays in Dublin with friends of the family and the time he turned up at his cousins' house for a five-day holiday while armed with seven boxes of Weetabix lest he wouldn't be fed, this was Rams's first proper holiday.

A hostel in Newport was to accommodate the students for three nights, with plenty of activities in nearby Westport and the surrounding areas keeping them occupied during the day.

It was a fine spring morning when the tour bus left Oldcastle for Mayo. Everyone was in good spirits and looking forward to the trip ahead. Unfortunately, things took a turn for the worse when the bus was about an hour away from its destination. Fingering Joe was feeling quite poorly, so some of the lads advised him to get the bus driver to pull up at the side of the road if he thought he was going to vomit. By the time Joe got his finger out and started for the top of the coach, it was too late; he couldn't contain it and, as several students ducked for cover, Joe projectile vomited in the middle of the aisle. Suddenly the bus ascended a steep slope and, in doing so, caused Joe's alarmingly abundant puke to flow down the bus aisle like a mudslide. The girls started screaming, the boys laughing, and the teachers roaring at them all to shut the hell up. The driver eventually stopped the bus and, learning of the situation, produced a mop with which Joe could clean up his mess.

The stench was so putrid that the Rams could only liken it to the time a few years earlier when Gavin O'Dowd let out a particularly devastating fart on the Munterconnaught primary school bus, causing Sean to evacuate everyone from the vehicle until the smell had subsided. Meanwhile Dowd could be seen running down the lane to his house with a huge smile on his face, obviously pleased with his unprecedented achievement.

The tour bus pulled into the hostel in Newport; Joe's incident almost forgotten amid the mass excitement. Each of the students in turn climbed into the back trunk of the coach, grabbing their luggage while avoiding the mop, which was hanging from the inside of the luggage compartment, puke dripping from it over several of the bags.

Everyone ran for the hostel in the hope of snaring one of the better bedrooms. The Rams was keen on sharing with the same lads he'd travelled to Dublin with two weeks earlier.

World Championship Wrestling had made a rare appearance at the Point Theatre, giving the Rams and Mara a unique chance to see in person the wrestlers they had been emulating in the schoolyard. The show took place on 17 March, so the organisers christened it 'The St. Patrick's Day Bash'. Stano and the All-Irishman, Big Ron, had also purchased tickets along with Ron's father, John, who drove the lads to and from the show. Derek Gavin, or Gavin for short, won two tickets in a newspaper competition, allowing him to join the others on the trip along with his younger brother Niall.

Since Gavin had won his tickets in a competition, the Rams presumed that Gavin's seats would be closer to ringside than his own. Therefore, he persuaded Niall to swap tickets. It would be an understatement to say that Rams was mildly disgusted when he discovered that Niall and the other lads were closer to the ring than he and Gavin. Nonetheless, the boys sat back and enjoyed a terrific event; culminating with Big Van Vader regaining the heavyweight title from Sting in the main event.

With the final match over, one would have expected that everyone would grab their jackets and start for home. Not so on this occasion. While Vader was walking towards the dressing room, Stano, Mara and the Ronster made a beeline for the ring. The Rams, from his lofty perch some rows behind, was quick to follow suit with Gavin in tow.

By the time the lads hit the ring there were at least three dozen like-minded strangers beating the living shite out of each other from post to post. The Rams eagerly began dropping elbows from off the top rope; Mara could be seen powerbombing a man who wasn't a day under 50 and Stano, with a 'Stinger' transfer across his face, had Ron locked into the Scorpion Death Lock manoeuvre. Unfortunately, within minutes several security personnel entered the fray, forcing the boys to retreat to John Tuite's waiting getaway car.

Things were similarly chaotic in Newport as close to 50 screaming boys and girls ran towards the hostel doors, arms outstretched and legs moving faster than they had in a long time.

After throwing his luggage onto a bottom bunk bed in one of the rooms, the Rams surveyed his surroundings, and was pleased to see that he was sharing with Stano, Ron, Terry and Gavin. Niall Keoghan, who was nicknamed Boo Boo after Yogi Bear's infamous sidekick, snagged the last bed.

Mayo—the Rams would soon learn—was the rain capital of the world; it certainly was when he visited. Shortly after arriving, and back on the tour bus again, a tour guide who one could only describe as being the female version of the former Guns N' Roses guitarist, Slash, boarded the bus to tell the group, 'It doesn't always rain in Mayo.'

'Could have fooled me,' chipped in the Rams.

The almost relentless rain put a dampener on the outdoor activities, but that didn't stop the kids from enjoying themselves. The second day of the tour saw them taking to a river in canoes. The Rams was one of a handful of students who couldn't swim. He had tried his hand at it a number of times but with little success. Swimming lessons took place daily each summer for two weeks at Lough Ramor, a medium sized lake that separated Munterconnaught from Virginia. But Growney's Wood ran parallel to the lake, offering the Rams the perfect playground from where he would often forgo the all-important swimming lessons to act the lad with some of the other boys—fighting with sticks, climbing trees and generally running amok. While in primary and secondary school, weekly lessons at Kells swimming pool didn't serve the Rams any better. He could swim lengths of the pool faster than Michelle De Bruin but, without his beloved floats, he was always a drowning victim in waiting.

On the river in Mayo, it turned out that Gavin couldn't swim to save his life either so rather than being stuck up shit creek without a paddle he and the Rams opted for the safe choice of a paddle boat instead of a canoe. The rest of the kids might have been laughing but Rams didn't care. He just sat back, expecting Gavin to man the ship. With Gavin seemingly as disinterested in steering the boat as Rams was, it wasn't long before strong winds carried the two lazy bastards down the river, leaving them almost out of view from the rest of the class.

Declaring a May Day alert, Gavin gestured towards Eddie who was one of the accompanying teachers on the trip. As Eddie approached the riverbank, the two lads jumped ship, stepping into the shallow water while holding onto the boat by an attached rope. Eddie beckoned the boys to bring the boat back up the river from where they could easily take it out of the water.

But by this stage Gavin was in trouble. He didn't much care for the stones that were cutting into his feet from the riverbed, so he stood rooted to the spot, forcing Eddie to switch into Mitch Bucannon mode. Removing his sandals and rolling his trouser legs up to his knees, he waded up to Gavin, offering him a piggyback to the nearby wall that was but 12 feet away. All the while, the Rams lugged the boat behind them, laughing at the site of Gavin's weight almost breaking Eddie's back.

As the weather worsened in the afternoon, the class went on an orienteering trip. Ever the height of fashion, the Rams was sporting a t-shirt with a blue see-through raincoat over it that was about as much use as a bin liner, and indeed a bin liner may well have looked better. Looking like a reject from *Joseph and the Amazing Technicolour Dreamcoat*, Rams wasn't surprised by the onslaught of smart remarks from the lads, especially since he had suffered somewhat of a wardrobe malfunction the previous night.

Since the Rams wasn't exactly a renowned traveller, it wasn't surprising that he didn't possess a sleeping bag. But the students had been advised to bring one on the tour. Therefore, Rams's mother landed home with a large sleeping bag in hand just hours before the tour was due to set off. It was rolled up tightly with a strong cord holding it in place. Since a relative had loaned it, the Rams believed there was no need to check that it was okay and would serve his purposes.

The following evening all of the students had retired to their rooms for the night. As the Rams began to unroll his sleeping bag, he realised that all was not as it seemed. To his horror, he discovered that the bag had grown arms and was more akin to an Eskimo coat than something that might suffice as bedding. Before Rams had a chance to hide the death trap, eagle-eyed Terry spotted it and was quick to alert the rest of the boys, all of whom then took turns to traipse around the room in what might have appeared to the untrained eye as being a yeti costume. Fortunately for the Rams, there was sufficient bed linen on his bed, so he quickly wrapped his outfit back up in the cord that had constrained it all the way to Mayo.

Rams probably should have worn his sleeping bag instead of the flimsy raincoat and t-shirt that he continued to wear during the following day's orienteering trip. Doing so might have prevented him from picking up a terrible flu, which he brought home with him to Cavan along with some fine memories and self-promises to, in future, distrust Slash look-alikes who try to downplay the weather in Mayo.

Chapter 9

DANCING, TURNING, PICKING

THERE COMES a time in every young man's life when the need arises for him to take those initial tentative steps onto the bottom rungs of the career ladder. For the Rams, those needs arose at the tender age of 15.

It was the summer of 1993 and a year that would prove to be a formative one in the young Rams's life. He had been attending junior discos for a few years, but over-18 venues were the holy grail of socialising for any boy of that age. Since his sister, Vanessa, had done all the pleading to their parents two years earlier to allow her to attend such discos, the Rams found things to be considerably easier when his time came. Therefore, he and Mara were amongst the first students in their year to attend Carraig Springs disco on a Sunday night in June 1993.

Carraig Springs was located in Crosskeys in Co. Cavan and, aside from the disco and adjoining bar, there wasn't a whole lot else to see in the area; no town, no bustling streets – just chip vans selling all manner of dodgy fast food to the drunk youths emerging from the club at all hours.

Although the Springs was located in the middle of nowhere, it attracted huge crowds from nearby towns such as Ballyjamesduff, Virginia and Oldcastle, making it one of the biggest night clubs in the country. Meatloaf, Boyzone and The Corrs, amongst others, played gigs there at one time or another. Unlike most other discos at the time, the dance floor was always heaving from about 9 o'clock until closing time.

Despite being but 15 years old, the Rams found it relatively easy to get past the bouncers at Springs. All he needed was one terribly dodgy fake ID, and the world—or in this case the Springs—would be very much his oyster.

Most underage teens attempting to sneak into a reasonably strict nightclub would have been content to own an ID stating that they had just turned 18 and, to be fair to him, so would the Rams. His supplier, however, wasn't forthcoming with the perfect ID, and so it came to pass that the Rams showed up at Springs with a Department of Education card that had his photo glued to it, was wrapped in cling film and stated that he had been born in 1969, which would have made him 24 years old. Unbelievably, following just a brief interrogation, he gained access to the club, proving that the bouncers would let anyone with a ridiculous ID through the doors.

A case in point involved Mara's 15 year old neighbour who appeared at Springs one night with a homemade college ID in his possession. It might have looked somewhat official had the name of the college been spelt correctly instead of 'Dublin Citie Univercitie'.

Well actually it still would have looked like the work of a two year old since the photograph stuck to the ID was not a passport-sized photo but an extremely obvious shot of a young boy on his confirmation day some years earlier. The photo had been 'cleverly' cropped so that the bishop's hand could barely be seen resting on the boy's shoulder. Apparently, the bouncers were laughing so much upon viewing the ID that the young lad managed to sneak past them into the club, delighted that he had put one over on 'those stupid bouncers'.

The Rams soon realised that going out to discos didn't come cheap. Although he was only drinking coke at the time, such minerals, along with buses and food, cost plenty of money. Therefore, it was obvious that he had to get his hands on a few pounds other than the bit of weekly pocket money he received from his parents. At the time, Rams's father, Jimmy, was working for a German family in Mountnugent, but some weekends he'd earn extra money working nearby for a man by the name of Sam Walker.

Sam was in his fifties, always full of chat, and his stories often made for good entertainment. He owned some land and a few turf plots on a bog close to his home. With the Rams crying out for work, Sam agreed to Jimmy's request to give his son a few days' work turning turf.

Working in the bog, the Rams discovered, was a right bastard of a job. It involved lifting sods of turf and stacking them so that the warm air circulating between the piled-up sods would in time make them fit for fuel. Obviously this necessitated a hell of a lot of bending down to lift the turf, resulting in one very sore back come the end of the working day. Add to that the long hours, isolation and hungry midge flies, and one mightn't have been surprised if the Rams didn't show up for a second day of gruelling punishment. But he was no quitter, and show up he most certainly did. After all, he needed the money and although he was only earning about 15 pounds per day, it was considerably more cash than his pocket money allowance. In any case, the amount of turf that needed turning dictated that there was no more than a few days work ahead and, as Rams's mother would often say, 'A little hard work never killed anyone.'

After all the turf had been turned and allowed to dry thoroughly for a few weeks, the Rams was back in the bog to bag the sods, load them onto a trailer and off-load them again at Sam's house. Jimmy and a local man, Tony, were also present so that the work would take no longer than a day. Everything was going fine until a gust of wind blew a considerable amount of dust into Jimmy's left eye.

Rubbing the afflicted eye only irritated it more, and before long it was welded shut. Jimmy decided he'd have to go home, but not before Doctor Tony came over to inspect the patient.

'Which eye is it, Jimmy?'

Maybe Tony had been partially blinded by the dust himself, but even Stevie Wonder should have been able to spot the eye in question.

'The one that's fucking closed, Tony,' growled Jimmy, thinking that Tony was taking the piss.

Jimmy eventually drove home with one eye watching the road, and the other eye not arsed in helping out. Once all of the turf reached its destination, Sam dropped the Rams home. Having truly earned the first few pounds of his life, Rams knew that things could only get easier; but would they?

Third Year in secondary school kicked off the following September. But unfortunately any money earned during the summer was long gone by October. Therefore, when Mara mentioned to the Rams that there was a few days' work available nearby picking potatoes, he jumped at the opportunity.

The money on offer was a measly 10 pounds a day and the employer was Des Hand, a local farmer who lived just outside Oldcastle. Along with the Rams, several other boys had taken time off school to work long hours for three days and little reward.

Des could crack a joke with the best of them, but the Rams soon realised it was a different story when working for him. Time was money and there was no time for anything else but, to be fair to Des, he had a living to make and, if the work fell behind schedule, he still had to pay the wages of close to 10 people.

Picking spuds, the Rams discovered, wasn't a million miles away from his turf-turning endeavours some months earlier. The biggest difference was that he was against the clock as he had to have his section of the field cleared of spuds in the time it took Des to drive to the far end of the field in the tractor and return to where he was picking. The potato harvester would then dig up more of the ground in front of the Rams, and the laborious process would continue.

Rams and Des didn't really get along from the get go. Potato picking isn't exactly brain surgery; bend down, pick up spuds and place them in large sack. Unfortunately, nobody told the Rams how many spuds should go in a sack. So, not wanting to waste any, he filled each one to the top until spuds were almost falling out onto the ground.

Everything seemed okay until later that afternoon when Des detached the potato harvester from the tractor and hooked up the trailer in its place. He then drove along to where each of the workers had been picking for the day, and together they loaded the spuds onto the trailer. Unbeknownst to the Rams, everyone else had only half-filled each sack, thus enabling easy loading. And whereas all the other sacks lay sporadically all over the field, the Rams had gone to the trouble of placing his in a line that was straighter than any road in Cavan.

Upon reaching the Rams, Des hopped out of the tractor and marched towards him. Unfortunately, it wasn't to congratulate him on creating the world's longest straight line comprised from loaded potato sacks, although the Rams probably felt that it should have been.

'How the fuck are we supposed to get those bags onto the trailer?' roared Des.

For once, the Rams was in a charitable humour and decided to hold back on the smart reply he was very tempted to unleash. Instead, he made an attempt to lift one of the sacks, but he only managed to move it two inches off the ground, which wasn't much use considering how much higher the trailer was. In the end, much to Des's annoyance, it took the mightiest of efforts from three of the lads to lift each bag onto the trailer.

Things went a little better on day two but, by the third and final day, the Rams made sure that he wasn't likely to run away with the 'Employee of Week' award.

Des was adamant that all of the work had to be complete by day's end, and his temperament was such that if anything hampered his plan, he was likely to transform from Bruce Banner to the Hulk in a matter of seconds.

As it happened, the lads only had to wait until just after lunch before the Hulk made a guest appearance. Des was driving along the field digging up the spuds when, all of a sudden, the tractor conked out. Many 'F' and 'C' expletives followed, along with something derogatory about our Lord's mother.

Two hours later Des was still lying under the tractor attempting to get the 'God damn piece of shite' working. By now, his face was redder than a tomato, and the lads knew to keep their distance and thus retreated to the far end of the field.

During this unexpected break from work, Rams's mind began wandering and he started thinking about how he might wind Des up. Since

Des was now fit to explode, the timing couldn't have been any better. He walked the 50 metres to where Des's head was just about visible under the tractor, knelt down and—with the lads listening—let fly with a short one-liner.

'Do you need a HAND there, HAND?'

Des banged his head off the underside of the tractor and began insulting our Lord's mother again as the Rams walked back to the lads.

'I think he said he can manage himself,' he said cheekily.

Fortunately for the Rams's well being, the tractor was up and running less than five minutes later and with not a moment to spare Des resumed harvesting the spuds while throwing the odd dagger-like stare towards the Rams whenever he could. Unsurprisingly, the Rams didn't return nor was he invited back to Hand's farm again. And chances are that neither man lost much sleep over it.

Chapter 10

SHAME ON YOU, RAY HOUGHTON

R AY HOUGHTON has a lot to answer for. Sure, he is an Irish soccer legend who famously put the ball in the English net, but he's also partly responsible for one of the biggest drinking sessions in Irish history.

It was June 1994 and, with just one final exam to sit in the Junior Certificate, the Rams and his mates were already in party mood. Rams and Mara had been attending discos at Springs for almost a year, and now Stano, Terry and Boo Boo were also on board, meaning they all potentially had a great summer of partying ahead of them.

The football World Cup had kicked off, and the Irish team faced a daunting challenge in their opening match against Italy at the Giant's stadium in New York. The game was to take place on a Saturday evening Irish-time, and it was to be broadcast live on a big screen at Springs, with a disco to follow. The lads hopped on a mini-bus in town, and arrived at Springs early enough to secure a table with a decent view of the screen.

First they had to get past the bouncers. Normally this wasn't a problem, only this time there were two gardai inspecting ID cards at the door. The Rams had a bit of a predicament on his hands because his precious fake ID had been confiscated by a bouncer on a recent visit to the club, and now he didn't know how he was going to gain entry.

Fortunately, Lady Luck was in town that night and so was Paschal Baugh. Paschal was a fellow Munterconnaught man, in his mid-twenties, and a hell of a sound fella to boot. He had been playing with his popular band, Abinitzio, in the lounge bar of the Springs that evening, and was packing some of the band equipment into his car when the Rams spotted him. He quickly darted over to Paschal and, following a few minutes of small talk, asked if he could borrow some form of ID from him that would help him get past the gardai. Ever the obliging chap, Paschal rummaged through his wallet, but only managed to produce a blood donor card, which had nothing but his name on it.

'That will do. Cheers Paschal,' said the Rams, and he rejoined the queue for the nightclub.

When the Rams reached the top of the queue, the local Sergeant greeted him and pulled him aside for the obligatory interrogation.

'Could I see some form of identification please?'

The Rams searched through his wallet for a few moments before calmly replying.

'I seem to have left my ID at home, Sergeant. All I have is this blood donor card.'

'There's no date of birth on this card,' growled the Sergeant in an attempt to rain on Rams's parade.

'Ah, but you have to be at least 18 to carry one of these cards,' grinned the Rams, pleased that he had surely put the Sergeant back in his box.

'Is that right? Tell me Paschal; where are you from?'

'Munterconnaught.'

'Easy question,' thought the Rams. *'Keep them coming.'*

'Have you any brothers or sisters?'

Now this was a strange one. The Rams didn't know the Baugh family well. Paschal was the youngest in the family. He had an older brother, Damien, but that was about as much as Rams knew about the Baugh family tree. Nevertheless, surely any answer would suffice in order to appease the Sergeant.

'Just the one brother, Damien.'

'And what's your mother's name?'

'Fucked if I know. But sure I'm on a roll here. I might as well fill this lad full of shite.'

'Bridie, Sir.'

'Now you listen here, Son,' roared the Sergeant. 'I know the Baugh family very well. I know Paschal and all of his many brothers and sisters. I even know his mother. Hell, I could probably tell you what the Baughs had for breakfast this morning. I'm warning you now. If you ever darken this door again, you'll be in a whole heap of trouble.'

Having confiscated the donor card, the Sergeant proved that he wasn't a complete ogre by allowing Rams into the club, despite his deceitfulness.

'Jaysis, it's a small old world,' said the Rams, stating the obvious as he rejoined his friends at a table close to the dance floor. Shortly thereafter, the DJ began fuelling the soccer frenzy with classic Irish football songs such as *Put 'em under pressure* and *Give it a lash Jack*. Rams was the only one amongst his group not drinking beer. Most of the lads had recently begun experimenting with drink, but Rams was holding tight—at least for the time being.

Mara began guzzling back the pints with the thirst of a well-parched camel and, by the time the pre-match coverage started, he was as pissed as a fart. Spirits were high throughout the nightclub as the match got underway. Italy may have been the hot favourites, but you can never count out the Irish. With only 11 minutes gone in the match, Houghton intercepted an attempted clearance from Baresi and then, from 40 yards out, he quickly turned and fired an incredible shot over the head of the out-of-position Pagliuca. Everyone in the Springs, along with every other man, woman and child in the country, began screaming in an unparalleled and unified moment of euphoria. As the time ticked by, Ireland's other hero of the day, Paul McGrath, played out of his skin to help his country secure a historic win. Once again and, not for the last time that night, *Put 'em under pressure* and *Give it a lash Jack* reverberated throughout the club. People were dancing all over the place, sworn enemies became best friends for the night, and there wasn't a single soul failing to contribute to the electric atmosphere.

A large puddle of vomit consumed an area close to where the lads had been sitting. It wasn't the watery type of puke one might associate with over-consumption of alcohol. Instead, it looked like someone had been mixing cement and poured it onto the floor. It was obviously the creation of some gobshite or other who had opted for chips and a few burgers before taking more drink on board than they could handle.

Undetected by Mara, the cement mix seemed to be drawing him closer to it as he danced a drunken dance that no man had ever seen before or would like to see again. In no time, Sean George was gyrating atop the puddle and, as people ran for cover in case they'd be splashed amid the horrific jig, he slipped in the mess, covering himself from head to toe in the vomit. Puking over oneself is never good, but dressing in someone else's regurgitated dinner is just inexcusable. Nonetheless, Mara seemed unaffected and, getting to his feet, he continued the dance that was—because of the fall—now more gross than it was entertaining.

As the madness ensued throughout the club, the Rams decided that he'd bite the bullet and sample some alcohol. With money constraints at the back of his mind, he decided to take a swig or two from Boo Boo's bottle of Heineken and, once that went down okay, he made for the bar to buy his first beer.

That infamous night in Springs in June 1994 marked the beginning of a long era of drinking sessions that would take the lads to many strange towns, resulting in numerous eventful and often hilarious adventures. Shame on you, Ray Houghton; you set the wheels in motion for all that followed.

Chapter 11

A NEW AND MATURE RAMS

WITH THE Junior Cert exams behind him, the Rams found himself in Fifth Year of secondary school, thereby officially making him a senior. But that didn't mean he was about to start acting like one.

Having performed well in the exams, Rams was attending all honours classes. When forced to make a decision on which optional subjects to study, he decided that French, Business Organisation and Biology would be of more use to him than practical subjects such as Engineering and Technical Drawing, which most of his friends had opted for. The Rams was one of only a few boys attending these classes, but fortunately two of his mates were amongst the male minority.

Stephen Gammell and Tommy Grall were two of the smartest kids in the school. Without breaking a sweat, Stephen had managed to obtain five As and five Bs in the Junior Cert. He was attentive in class, but didn't spend too much time staring into books because his naturally high IQ dictated that he didn't have to. The Rams figured that Gammell could have been a distant relative of Dustin Hoffman's autistic character from the movie *Rain Man* because, like Raymond Babbitt, one quick scan of a chapter in a book would often be enough to permanently embed the information into Gammell's brain. Not sure how good he was at counting spilled toothpicks though!

Tommy was also a bit of a whiz kid. Although Mathematics had once been one of Rams's favourite classes, Tommy's knowledge of the subject must surely have rivalled that of Pythagoras. Rams claimed to have lost interest when, 'they took the numbers out of it' and, as Mara acutely observed one day in conversation, 'The only time you a see a number in Maths classes these days is when you look at the page numbers of the book.'

Gammell and Tommy were also in the same Mathematics class as the Rams who, despite now being a senior, perceived the changes from his Junior Cert days to be minimal. Paddy Traynor now taught him Maths instead of Science, and Rams still gave him stick despite the lack of a large audience. In fact there were only five students in the class, some of whom didn't always appreciate the near constant distractions.

As was the case in the past, after enduring several minutes of needless ribbing, Paddy would eventually lose the rag in a more expressive manner than ever before.

'Good God almighty; Raymond or Ronan. By God, I have kids at home and they're only seven or eight and, by Jesus, they have more sense than ya.'

This part of Paddy's speech was the same as ever, although his children were now two or three years older. But then his rant would continue into a director's cut version.

'You're like a hen in a criddle and a bull in the mist. You just don't seem to give a fiddler's dab what's going on here.'

Now the Rams wasn't entirely sure what a criddle was and he sure as hell didn't have a clue what a fiddler's dab might be, but he sort of garnered from Paddy's raised voice that neither attribute was commendable. Fortunately, it was only a matter of seconds before Paddy cooled down and the class resumed until the next inevitable interruption.

In Physical Education classes, things were the same as usual. Rams continued to be sent off from every sport imaginable, and it soon got to the stage where he was almost as pissed off with his disciplinary record as Colgan was. Rather than waste his own time each week togging out for maybe five minutes' exercise, he asked his mother to write a note to Colgan conveying that he had a bad back and wouldn't be able to partake in any sports for a few weeks.

Colgan read the note and accepted it at face value. More notes followed over the course of the next few weeks and, any time Rams didn't bring one with him, Colgan would question his absence from class and the legitimacy of his injury. He would then attempt to put her firmly in her place by saying, 'Ah, the auld back is acting up. Sure you know how it is yourself', in a reference to her rumoured bad back, which supposedly prevented her from doing anything more strenuous in class than blowing a whistle. Colgan, pissed off over that sneaky dig, would reply, 'No, I don't know how it is, Ronan.' She'd then walk away with her head held low, defeated once again by her smart-assed protagonist.

Despite being unsure as to whether his back would ever fully recover, the Rams's condition took a miraculous turn for the better every time soccer returned to the P.E. curriculum. Telling Colgan that, 'The back is greatly improved this week, Miss', he'd return to the field in dramatic fashion, shouting and roaring and sometimes earning more red cards to go with the others. As soon as footy was off the class agenda, however, the Rams's ongoing injury would mysteriously sideline him again.

Colgan, eventually realising that she was being taken for a fool, demanded that the Rams produce a doctor's note diagnosing this on-again off-again injury. A curt letter from Rams's mother followed, in which she stated that such a note would be forthcoming as soon as the school coughed up the money necessary to obtain one. The money never materialised so neither did the doctor's note, the absence of which—much to Colgan's dismay—left the Rams free to partake in P.E. whenever he pleased.

While Colgan had her hands full with the Rams, other teachers had an equally torrid time trying to maintain order in the classroom when he was present. Things worsened when Rams and Goosey shared the same class.

Geography was one of a handful of classes where the Rams found himself reunited with his old friends, Goosey and Stano. Stano was prone to long spells of studious behaviour where one could almost swear he was the most angelic student in the class. Other days, he'd annoy the teachers more than the Rams could ever manage and, as a result, he'd pay the price with a detention or two. Rams and Goosey were also somewhat well behaved in certain classes, but Geography wasn't one of them.

Mrs. Sheridan, the Geography teacher, was an intelligent woman who obviously knew her subject matter extremely well, but she was the proud owner—according to the Rams—of the 'world's most boring voice'. This voice, he claimed, drove him to distraction and caused him to do anything but listen to it during classes. Goosey was of a similar opinion, and was in the enviable position of being the best in the class at Geography, which meant he could afford more than anyone else to act the fool.

Goosey's little quirks were now even more evident than in the days when he ran around picking up cows' shite. He had recently become the proud owner of arguably the most unique wasp collection known to mankind. To the untrained eye, it looked like an ordinary copybook, but inside its pages laid the squashed remains of dozens of wasps, which had over the course of months or even years been carefully glued into place with correction fluid. It made for a slightly grotesque sight, with guts and wings on every page making it difficult to distinguish where one wasp's body ended and the next began.

Being smarter at Geography than even Gammell meant that Goosey's homework in the subject was high in demand. It wasn't uncommon for students to copy homework from each other prior to a teacher entering the classroom, and some had perfected the act into an art form.

Knowing how much his collection freaked out the girls in the class, Goosey couldn't resist playing a trick on one of them when the opportunity presented itself. Katie Sheedy seldom had her homework completed and, for the first five minutes of every Geography class, she could usually be seen copying the previous night's exercises. She was also of a rather delicate disposition and, when she borrowed what she thought was Goosey's Geography copybook one day, she got more than she bargained for.

As Mrs. Sheridan rattled on about meandering rivers in the arse hole of nowhere, a highly pitched scream reverberated throughout the small room as Katie bolted from her seat and, in a puff of smoke, shot out the door of the class while screaming, 'Wasps, wasps; there's loads of them.'

The December snow on the ground outside suggested that there was a greater chance of Rams winning a 'Student of the Year' award than a swarm of wasps invading the classroom. Then, without even lifting her head from the book she was reading, Mrs. Sheridan implied as much.

'Well it is the weather for them all right,' she noted and continued reading; obviously assuming that Katie had taken leave of her senses.

While Goosey's other copybooks weren't portable wasp museums, they did serve a use by providing him with a source of nutrition when hunger came calling, which usually occurred in the Geography class just before lunchtime each Tuesday. Goosey would tear an entire page from one of his copybooks and then roll it into a ball, place it in his mouth and begin chewing while Mrs. Sheridan would try her best to ignore this unusual and distracting act. As she'd read aloud from the Geography book, the class would read silently along with her, turning the pages every few minutes.

Meanwhile the Rams's Geography book resembled something that had gone through a washing machine on more than a few occasions and then been dragged by horses from one end of the country to the other. As such, since he didn't believe it could look any worse than it did, he would rip each page out while turning it and would then place it carefully on top of all the other pages that had previously been pulled from the binding of the book. He knew that this juvenile act irritated the hell out of Mrs. Sheridan, so occasionally—just to be extra annoying—he would tear a page as slowly and loudly from the book as he could manage.

One day Mrs. Sheridan, no longer able to contain herself, launched an attack on the Rams, asking him if he knew how expensive books were and informing him that they don't just grow on trees to which the Rams gently reminded her that, 'In fact, technically books do grow on trees', and this led to a further five minute rant from Mrs. Sheridan about what a 'pup' the Rams was. As her temper subsided and silence dominated the room for what seemed like an eternity, the sound of paper tearing was to be heard. Mrs. Sheridan, about to blow another fuse, looked towards the Rams but he was the picture of innocence whereas Goosey, who was seated next to him, was hungry and no speech about disappearing rainforests was going to prevent him from tucking into a flavourless pre-lunch appetiser. Mrs. Sheridan resigned herself to · ignoring the two and continued with the class. Some teachers knew when to accept defeat and she was one of them.

The fact that Rams and Goosey were more intelligent than they let on to be was perhaps part of the reason why many teachers put up with their immature behaviour, hoping that they might come good in the end. Both students excelled at English, but unfortunately Goosey's messing in class in the run up to the Junior Cert exams had conspired against him so that when he began Fifth Year he found himself wrongly placed in the ordinary level class. Nonetheless, he continued to enjoy himself, bathing in the luxury of being top of the class.

One of Goosey's unique talents with regards to English was being able to, in a matter of seconds, compose a rude poem or story containing all of the names of the main characters from whatever play or novel the class was studying at the time. The poems served a duel purpose; they helped him remember the names of the characters for exam purposes, and they earned him a few laughs from his classmates.

Arthur Miller's *Death of a Salesman* was just one of a few pieces of respected literature reduced to nothing but a sordid sex tale in this manner.

Death of a Salesman Characters by Goosey
Biff is happy cause his Willy is Stanleying up for Linda who wants
Howard to Wagner but Miss Forsythe won't Letta with Uncle Ben.
'Bend'ard [Bernard] for me Charley,' shouts the Woman Waiter.

Goosey's masterpieces were never likely to win him a Booker prize but they did serve to further endear him to most of the class.

Nonetheless, when one is keeping one's nose clean is often the time that the shit hits the fan. Goosey would soon find this to be true.

Chapter 12

GET OUT, STAY OUT AND GET THE FIRE BRIGADE OUT

B RENDAN KENNEDY was a Religion teacher at St. Olivers. He was a quiet man who perhaps took himself and his subject matter too seriously, and this led to him becoming a major source of ribbing for some of his unruly male students.

Rams couldn't be bothered paying attention in a class that wouldn't feature in his Leaving Certificate Exams, so he particularly relished making Brendan's job as difficult as possible, and he found that he wasn't alone on this quest. During fifth and sixth year, the boys and girls were separated for Religion classes. While the girls' classes were a civilised affair, the boys spent the entirety of their lessons winding Brendan up.

One boy, Aidan Fitzpatrick, had a face in which Brendan could probably see Satan. He was known as Slug and, for a time, he sported an unprecedented Mohican haircut that made him a legend amongst his fellow students and a figure of hate and annoyance amongst the teachers. Each week Slug sat at the back of the class, refusing to complete even the simplest of exercises. Whenever Brendan ordered him to co-operate he would refuse, stating that he didn't believe in God. He knew that such a denouncement would really offend the religious zealot while simultaneously generating an abundance of laughter from his classmates.

Paul Halpin sat beside Slug. His obligatory nickname was Spade, and he was a bit of a loose cannon. He was renowned for getting into fights and, although he was well able to look after himself, he usually complemented his flying fists with all manner of makeshift weapons when on the war path.

One infamous combat tale involving Spade told of a fist fight he had with a local boy who, although a few years Spade's junior, had been looking for a fight one day after school. Spade swiftly sent the poor lad home with a bloody nose, but the boy tried to return the favour an hour later by arriving at Spade's house with all 24 stone of his fuming father in tow. The old man took a swing at Spade but missed and, before he had time to throw another punch, Spade calmly dug deep into his jacket pocket and produced a trowel, which he had made in Metalwork class some days earlier. He then used the weapon to beat the living daylights out of the father, gave the son another beating for good measure and sent the two of them running home for their lives.

While Brendan wasn't a violent character, he had previously—amidst moments of extreme provocation—lightly struck trouble-some students. Rams reckoned that if Brendan were to strike Spade, it would be the last thing he'd do. This almost came to pass one day when Spade and Slug were loudly denouncing God in unison, forcing Brendan to confront them at their desks. Foolishly, he grabbed Spade's arm and told him to behave himself. In response, Spade clenched a fist with his free hand and, in no uncertain terms, told Brendan to, 'Get your fucking hands off me or I'll kill ya.'

The expression on Spade's face left Brendan under no illusion that he was deadly serious. Quickly backing off, he returned to the top of the class, apparently realising that Spade wasn't one to be messed with. A few months later he learnt that Goosey was no soft touch either. Like his fellow Munterconnaught mates, Goosey was usually very easy going but, as the saying goes, 'Hell hath no fury like a Munterconnaught man scorned.'

It was a normal run-of-the-mill Religion class aside from the fact that on this day Brendan was being provoked more than usual and seemed to be cracking under the pressure. He told the boys to pray for several minutes while keeping their heads resting on the desks in front of them. Goosey was one of a minority of individuals who bothered his arse obeying Brendan's wishes, and he sat quietly with his forehead almost touching his desk as some of the other boys behind him sat upright with little or no interest in praying. A few of them began making squeaking noises, and Brendan must have become convinced that Goosey was amongst the guilty party because he immediately rushed to where he was sitting. But, just as he reached Goosey, Brendan appeared to slip and accidentally slammed Goosey's head into the desk where he had been praying.

Goosey, thinking he had been attacked, sprung to his feet with a head like a bull on him.

'Ya fuckin' bollocks ya. What did ya do that for? Pick a fuckin' window there cause you're going through one of them,' he said, pointing at the three panes of glass at the side of the room from which Brendan was expected to choose one for his imminent defenestration. Brendan was still trying to explain the slippage when Goosey stormed out of the room, vowing never to return.

One person who was seldom at the receiving end of a bruising—accidental or otherwise—was Sean George Mara II. Over the years, many people had found any sort of physical attack on Mara to be ineffectual and likely to be met with a big grin, which in turn could induce more pointless violent attacks from the aggressor.

Back in First Year, shortly after Mara ran Donny Farrelly out of the Ceili House, Peter McCabe tried to do likewise to Sean George. Peter, who was the senior barman, had to endure occasional smart-assed remarks from Rams and Mara while they were playing pool at lunchtime, but he usually coped admirably by issuing a few harmless jibes of his own.

One day the Rams noticed that the coin receiver on the pool table was dodgy and, by pushing it in and gently holding it in position, he could get four or five games of pool for the price of one. Unfortunately, after a few weeks, Peter figured out what the boys were up to and attempted to throw them out—literally.

He went for Mara first and, following several failed attempts at pushing him towards the door, put him in a headlock and dragged him outside. Mara might have resisted but he was too busy convulsing in laughter at the very idea of Peter throwing him out.

Peter then focused his attention on the Rams, attempting to deploy the same methods of eviction that had worked so successfully on Sean George. But Rams possessed a renowned 'lethal grip', whereby if he decided to take a hold of something, it would take a small army to budge him. Having locked his arms around a pillar, Rams stood firm as Peter tried in vain to move him. He soon realised that the Rams was going nowhere, so he reluctantly released him from the headlock and backed off. Rams then stepped away from the pillar, dusted himself off and joined Mara outside, telling him that he had, 'let Peter off with a warning'.

Fortunately, Oldcastle wasn't short of a pub or two, and it would take some effort from the lads to get barred from all of them. Nevertheless, it seemed that they were more than up to the task. Over the next few years the group of lads gathering to play pool each day grew in number, and usually included Rams and Mara with part-time members Stano, Terry, Gammell and Tommy.

With the Ceili House's doors closed to the boys, they began frequenting the Mountain Dew bar on a daily basis. Initially the barman, Eamon, didn't object to the reasonably large group of lads surrounding the pool table, shouting and cursing as if there wasn't a sinner in sight. But when one or two customers, unable to enjoy a quiet pint, left their drinks on the counter and walked out of the pub, Eamon was visibly vexed. Rather than initiating a confrontation with the unruly group, he waited until the following day and, as soon as the boys walked into the bar, he told them that the pool table was out of order. When the lads returned a day later, only to be told that the floor was about to be hovered, they knew that Eamon was indirectly attempting to bar them from the premises. Upon arriving the next day, a yarn from Eamon about the cue ball being missing confirmed their suspicions.

Not ones to be bested, the lads reappeared the following Monday afternoon and slotted money into the pool table before Eamon had a chance to draw breath. As they began their first game, Rams and Stano couldn't resist conversing very loudly between each other, mainly for Eamon's benefit.

'Jaysis, Stano. We were lucky to get a game of pool today, what with there being no light bulb above the table and all,' remarked the Rams.

Stano burst out laughing, but quickly regained his composure to reply.

'You're right, Rams. And there's no chalk either. Sure how did we get playing at all?'

'Wait lads,' roared the Rams at the top of his voice. 'There's no beer mats laid out on the tables over there. Under these abysmal conditions, how can we possibly dedicate ourselves to the sport we love?'

Eamon was livid but appeared to be biting his tongue for the time being. Just then, Mara began belching really loudly and, following each announcement, Rams would ask, 'What's that you're saying, Mara?' to which Sean George would reply with another euphonious burp.

No longer able to contain himself, Eamon started shouting the place down.

'Get out. Get the hell out of this pub now. And stay out.'

And so it was that the boys were rightly barred from a second pub in Oldcastle. Shortly thereafter, they made the Fincourt bar their venue of choice, this time keeping their shenanigans to a bare minimum and thus remaining there for the remainder of their school lunch breaks.

But not content with being thrown out of two pubs, the Rams managed to achieve a similar feat in a shop in Oldcastle on numerous occasions during his final year at St. Olivers.

Spice Street was a sweet shop located in the heart of the town. It was an ancient building, the foundations of which could well have been laid by the Vikings. The owners—like the shop they kept—were getting on a bit and seemed oblivious to the fact that they were sitting behind a public counter and not at home in front of the fire.

Ronny and Moe were cousins who were of American origin, had served in the Second World War, and bought Spice Street upon

settling in post-war Ireland. Moe was seldom seen in the shop so
Ronny worked the till most of the time. He sat permanently facing
a television in the corner of the shop, one eye permanently fixated
on *Oprah* and the other occasionally glancing across the shop to see
if anyone needed serving. At times forgetting—or perhaps not car-
ing—that he was at work, Ronny would wage a civil war on his left
or right nostril, using the sharp end of a pencil to dig those green terrorists out of there. One day the Rams walked into the shop just as a
giant scab flew past his nose. He looked across the counter, only to
see Ronny with his left trouser leg rolled up, the leg resting on the
Mars bars, and a Stanley knife grasped in his right hand as he scraped
off dead skin and old scabs from his body. As one might imagine, it
wasn't the manicured staff or the squashed confectionary that brought
the Rams into the shop after school each day. His main reason for being there was to play a video game called *Super Sidekicks 2*.

A few months earlier, Rams's family moved from Munterconnaught
to a new house in Virginia. Having spent most of his life in a small
and slightly damp albeit immaculately clean cottage, Rams was glad
to be moving to a larger house and, although that brought many ben-
efits with it, easy access to and from Oldcastle wasn't one of them.

Moving schools wasn't an option the Rams considered for even a
minute. Fortunately, one of his new neighbours worked in Oldcastle,
and he kindly provided Rams with a lift to school each morning. A
bus from Oldcastle to Virginia dropped Rams home in the evenings,
but it didn't depart the town until 5 o'clock, giving him quite a bit of
time to kill. Rather than waste this time by studying, the Rams would
always head for Spice Street.

Spice Street's main attraction was its three arcade machines. One of
the games available was a top-down shoot-em'-up, which Mara had
completed several times. Never boring of the repetitive nature of the
game, he eventually gave it a new lease of life by successfully playing
it while keeping both eyes firmly fixed on a mirror that was adjacent
to the machine. The second machine hosted a different game every
few months, but it was the ever-present *Super Sidekicks 2* in the third
machine that consistently entertained the crowds.

Super Sidekicks 2 was a simple football game with extremely addictive and entertaining qualities. Rams would normally drop into the shop for a game on his way back to school from the Fincourt. A small crowd gathered round the machine, shouting and cheering, would often signify a hotly-contested match was taking place.

Of all the people who regularly played *Sidekicks*, the Rams and David Fox were the two who excelled most at the game. This was primarily because they got an extra bit of practice after school hours when they would meet to play five or six games prior to Rams's bus arriving and Fox leaving for his evening job in the nearby supermarket.

Fox, like the Rams, was more vocal than most and could talk the talk all day long. Fox being Fox and Rams being Rams, there was little chance of both boys not shouting the odds when they met head-to-head for a game of *Super Sidekicks 2*. And shout they certainly did, especially during the most extreme moments of excitement.

'Ya hairy arsed hoor from Clontarf', was typical of what Fox would roar at the screen as the Rams's players dispossessed him, launching an attack on his goal. Rams used similar non-sensical and childish expressions mid-game, but saved his best ones for those rare occasions when he'd managed to score a winning goal just prior to the final whistle. Then the real tormenting would start.

'Yippedy yo, you're too slow', would be the initial insult, swiftly followed by, 'How do you know? Because the crowd went Hoooo.' If Fox looked especially disappointed over the loss, the Rams would attempt to lower his morale even further with one of his many other expressions.

'I've never had such an easy victory. That was like taking candy off a baby.'

As the games rolled on, the banter would reach the lowest depths of depravity imaginable, eventually turning Ronny from a quiet, soft-spoken man into a fist clenching anti-Christ. Either or both of the boys would be shown the door for offending Ronny's delicate senses, and told never to return. Fortunately, the barring order was usually lifted within 24 hours, leaving the two foul-mouthed footy fans to come up with new ways of insulting each other.

Having spent five years at St. Olivers, the Rams believed that the town of Oldcastle, just like Munterconnaught, felt very much like home. But the Leaving Certificate examinations were looming, the results of which would take the Rams away from home on a new journey to the last place he could have ever imagined.

Chapter 13

FATE TAKES OVER

SOME PEOPLE know from an early age what they want to do with their lives and they go on to pursue their dreams. Others spend years finding their way, with various levels of success, and a small number of people are fortunate enough to stumble upon the correct path after finishing secondary school. As luck would have it, the Rams belonged to the latter category and, despite his best efforts to sabotage his future, he managed to land on his feet when it came to securing a place on a suitable college course.

About 18 months prior to his Leaving Certificate examinations, Rams set his sights on going to UCD to study Arts. He was more than capable of attaining enough points to be offered a place on the course; 10 honours in the Junior Certificate exams were testament to what a motivated Rams could achieve. But about six months before the Leaving, Rams began to lose interest in his studies. His favourite subject, English, continued to receive his undivided attention, but at the expense of other subjects such as Biology.

Rams sat beside Stephen Gammell for Biology classes. It was the one subject the Rams felt he would never come to grips with, no matter how much work he put in. He didn't exactly help himself by spending every class talking to Gammell in an attempt to drive him to distraction. Rams reckoned if he was going down he might as well bring the brainiest student in the year with him. He didn't reckon, however, on his friend's multi-tasking abilities. Gammell would talk freely to the Rams during class, but he would also take in every word from the teacher's mouth, thereby ensuring that his studies wouldn't suffer.

One day, just a few short weeks before the exams were due to start, Mrs. Sheridan stood in for the Biology teacher who had taken ill earlier that day. She ordered the class to study for their exams but it wasn't long before the overbearing silence awakened the mischievous side of Rams's personality.

Katie Sheedy sat just in front of the Rams. She had become slightly withdrawn since the 'wasp incident' a year earlier and, such was her fear now of all creatures—dead or alive—she refused to partake in all animal-related experiments in Biology.

With Mrs. Sheridan's head buried in a book, the Rams sneaked down to the bottom of the class and began rooting through the presses. Within seconds, he had returned to his desk with several live worms in his possession and, before Gammell had a chance to say, 'What are ya at Rams?', the worms were perched atop Katie's head, somewhat camouflaged amongst her dark curly hair.

Moments later, upon sensing movement upstairs, Katie ran her fingers through her hair, discovered the unwelcome nest and burst into tears. As she ran from the classroom sobbing, 'Ah, there's worms in my hair', Mrs. Sheridan looked up from her book.

'Not this again,' she sighed as Katie's voice echoed throughout the corridors of the school, leading everyone but the Rams and Gammell to believe that she was barking mad.

The first week of June 1996 heralded the beginning of Rams's Leaving Certificate Exams and, one might have hoped, the cessation of the infantile messing for which he and several of his classmates were renowned. Irish was one of the first exams facing the students. As they took their places in the exam hall, the quiet chattering quickly gave way to the type of silence one could only associate with exams, with only the occasional rustling of papers adding any sign of life to the room.

Sean Smith sat two seats ahead of the Rams. Most people knew him as Jockey even though he had never sat on a saddle in his life.

Irish wasn't one of Jockey's favourite subjects so it wasn't surprising that, within minutes of the exam beginning, he was all but finished writing. Rather than leave the exam hall early, Jockey took it upon himself to provide some in-flight entertainment.

All of a sudden, a loud noise reverberated throughout the hall. It was instantly identifiable as a shotgun-type fart, but few people other than the Rams realised that it had emanated from Jockey. Several students couldn't help but laugh aloud and Rams was nearly in hysterics.

Farting is a funny old business. It's one of those rare acts that, depending on the situation, can either disgust or amuse the audience. On this occasion, both emotions were felt in equal measure amongst the students; some were laughing and others were visibly vexed that someone would dare distract them from such an important exam. The exam administrator didn't look overly amused either, but he remained silent, hoping the interruption had been a nervous once-off.

Five minutes later and Jockey was at it again. This time he fired four or five loud machine gun rounds from his arse. The Rams, who was still regaining his composure after several minutes of hysterical laughing, was now visibly crying in amusement at Jockey's announcement.

The administrator had heard and smelt enough.

'Whoever did that should be ashamed of themselves. What sort of an animal are you?' he bellowed.

He had no idea who the guilty party was but must surely have narrowed his investigation down to the area where the Rams could be seen struggling to stay in his seat as he threatened to laugh himself to death. A full 20 minutes elapsed before Rams managed to pull himself together to concentrate on the small matter of the exam he was supposed to be taking. The remainder of the exams passed without further incidents and, by the time the results were due, the Rams and a significant amount of his classmates were in Cork city to see *Oasis* playing live at Pairc Ui Chaoimh.

Getting to Cork from Cavan wasn't the most straightforward of routes without a car. The lads' travel plan involved getting a bus to Dublin, sinking a few pints when they got there and then taking another bus from the capital to Cork.

Upon arriving at the alienscape that was O'Connell Street in Dublin, the Rams was in desperate need of a toilet. Spotting a McDonalds nearby, he told the others to wait outside and he'd be back in a minute. As he swung the lavatory door open, his bladder was close to bursting. Fortunately, a stranger quickly moved aside and Rams took his place, relieved that his new Wranglers had been saved an embarrassing soaking.

As Rams rushed out the door to catch up with the lads, Mara who, unbeknownst to the Rams, had been in the lavatory at the same time as himself, was relaying to the others that he had just seen Rams urinating in a sink in McDonalds. Sure enough, in his hurried bid to relieve himself, Rams had mistakenly confused the new, fancy and weirdly-shaped sinks for urinals.

'Well, what the fuck are they doing making sinks that look like toilets?' was all that he could utter in his defence as his mates continued to take the piss out of him.

Eventually arriving in Cork for their three-day visit, the boys' expectations were certainly exceeded as enjoyable nights out and a smashing concert to boot made the long trip worthwhile. Not even a fire-induced middle of the night evacuation of the hostel they were staying in could dampen the boys' spirits, but separate phone calls each of them were to make on the last day of their stay threatened to do just that.

The Leaving Certificate results had been sent to all schools in the country while the boys were still in Cork. As such, Rams had sent his mother to retrieve his results in the morning, and he was to ring in the afternoon to find out how he had done. All of his mates had issued similar retrieval instructions to their parents.

As the Rams rang home from a busy city centre street, he was slightly nervous and somewhat concerned that his results would match the disinterest he had shown in the six months preceding the exams.

Rams's mother answered the phone in her new role as exam results announcer.

'Well, how did I do?' asked the Rams somewhat sheepishly.

'You did very well, you passed everything.'

The Rams couldn't believe he had passed Biology. The other grades were pretty much as expected, but surely Biology, the bane of his studies, had blemished his results.

'What did I get in Biology?' he enquired.

'The results on the sheet are in Irish, Ronan. Which one is Biology?'

'Bitheolaíocht, I think.'

'Oh, you got an E in that one.'

Rather than explaining that anything below a D was a fail mark, Rams rolled his eyes, cut the conversation short and began his celebrations with his friends. Fortunately, the E in Biology was irrelevant because he had sat seven exams, the results of his best six being all that would count towards him securing a place in college.

Upon arriving home the following day to examine his results, Rams realised that he had fallen well short of the points needed in order to be offered a place on the Arts course he had set his heart on months earlier. He had applied for several other courses but had no idea which ones because he'd pretty much picked courses that had fancy names, without giving them a second thought thereafter. When the college offers began arriving by post some days later, a place on a newly-created Multimedia course in Waterford RTC proved to be the most tempting. Rams accepted the offer and, shortly thereafter, word on where all his other friends would be going began filtering through.

Stano and Mara were Dundalk-bound; Gammell, Tommy, Terry and half of Oldcastle were offered places in various colleges and universities in Dublin, and there was a rumour circulating that Goosey—like the Rams—had been offered a place at Waterford RTC.

The Rams immediately got on the phone. During the conversation that followed, Goosey confirmed that, having attended primary and secondary school with the Rams, he would now be joining him in Waterford for their college years.

'What course is it, Goosey?' asked the Rams.

'Multimedia.'

Chapter 14

IT'S A LONG WAY FROM MUNTERCONNAUGHT

RAMS COULD scarcely believe it. In what was surely one of the biggest coincidences he'd ever heard of, both he and Goosey were set to attend the same course in college with neither party being aware of the other's fate prior to the revealing telephone conversation, which occurred that August evening.

Goosey also mentioned that Gavin O'Dowd would be commencing his second year at the same college in September and he had invited Goosey to move into a flat with him in the city. Dowd had already secured the accommodation for the year and, although Goosey was fairly sure that there were three beds in the flat, necessitating the sourcing of a third tenant, the vacancy wasn't his to fill and he advised Rams to contact Dowd directly if he was interested in moving in.

This would be the Rams's first time living away from home; so given the choice between moving in with strangers or sharing a flat with his friend of 13 years, his mind was already made up before Goosey had even finished talking. Nevertheless, there was a slight stumbling block and that was Dowd himself.

Rams and Dowd never had much time for each other during their primary school years. Dowd had been in the year ahead of the Rams and was only a few weeks older and, in hindsight, it was perhaps their similarities that served as a catalyst for their many feuds during that time. Like the Rams, Dowd was a notorious wiseacre but also extremely resourceful with his gift of the gab. As he grew older, he honed this God-given gift to infallible perfection yet, even at an early age, his crafty resourcefulness never failed to amaze those around him.

Dowd was one of dozens of Munterconnaught school kids who, while in primary school, frequented Growney's wood each summer for the swimming lessons at Lough Ramor. Getting to the lessons was a challenge in itself because the wood was located at the end of a mile-long, winding, narrow lane, which had more potholes than all of Cavan's other lanes and roads combined. Fortunately, the first quarter mile of the lane was in reasonable condition, and thereby easily traversable by bicycle, and Goosey's house was situated within that stretch. As such, it was common practice for some kids to cycle from their homes to Goosey's house, leave their bicycles at the back of his garage and face the rest of the journey on foot.

One day Dowd reached Goosey's house with just moments remaining before he was due to take a swimming test down at the lake. Not wanting to risk damaging his own bike, he secured it to a fence, changed into his swimming trunks and, spotting Rams's BMX, proceeded to jump on the saddle and cycle at full speed to Growney's Wood. Upon arriving there and, with no desire to dismount and walk the remaining few yards to the water's edge, he continued cycling until he landed himself and the bike into the lake just in time for him to begin his test. Once that was out of the way, lunch beckoned. Unfortunately for Dowd he had managed to forget his lunchbox amid his frenzied departure from the house that morning. But that didn't mean he would go hungry.

Rams, Goosey and Stano were sitting on a stretch of grass about to break bread when Dowd and his friend, Martin Brady, approached. Dowd began making small talk with the boys and, even though the Rams felt that this uncharacteristically friendly behaviour was camouflaging an impending prank, a further 10 minutes of benign banter made him think that he was being overly suspicious and should give Dowd the benefit of the doubt.

As the boys prepared once again to start eating lunch, Dowd

suddenly suggested that it would be a good idea for everyone to share their lunches, thereby ensuring that each of them would enjoy a varied meal. It was no secret that, at this stage in his life, Rams believed most types of sandwiches to be his enemy and so his lunch normally contained all manner of biscuits, chocolate bars and other savoury treats. For this very reason he was reluctant to swap any of his food for unimaginative, bland sandwiches, which inevitably inhabited the lunchboxes of the other boys. Unfortunately, he was out-voted four-to-one and thus forced to succumb to the whims of the group rather than looking like a parsimonious good-for-nothing.

One lunchbox at a time went round the group, each of the lads selecting a portion of food from it before passing it onto his nearest companion. This process continued until a lunchbox was devoid of its contents, at which time another open container was circulated. Dowd ate more than anyone else and his lunch, as was envisaged in his master plan, was to be the final one shared amongst the group. When his turn came, he stood up, pointed at something in the distance and, with the boys momentarily distracted, ran for his life in the opposite direction. Rams gave chase but Dowd's head start allowed him enough time to pull a wet dishevelled BMX from a nearby hedge and make good on his pre-planned escape.

'That's my bike,' was all the Rams could manage when he realised that the BMX he thought to be safely secured at Goosey's house was now moving further and further away from him with a sated Gavin O'Dowd atop the saddle.

After finishing primary school Dowd and Rams saw little of each other for several years as they were attending different secondary schools. Nonetheless, following his conversation with Goosey, the Rams was a little apprehensive as he dialled Dowd's phone number, wondering if their chequered history would ruin his chance of securing the final place in the flat in Waterford. As it happened, he needn't have been concerned because Dowd's voice conveyed warmth and genuine friendliness, and he heartily told the Rams that he was welcome to move into the flat.

Rams and Goosey made the laborious journey down to Waterford the week before Dowd was due to join them. The Rams had always falsely believed that Waterford was tucked just under Dublin. He soon found out, however, that it would take a three-hour-plus bus journey from the capital to get there. Those hours, combined with the trip from Cavan to Dublin, time queuing for said buses and other unforeseen delays, resulted in a five- to six-hour journey from his house to Waterford. As such, he decided that he would only venture home from college every three weeks.

Upon arriving at Waterford's main bus station, Rams and Goosey made their way by foot towards town. A medium-sized bridge separated the station from the outer parts of the city centre and, upon crossing it, the heart of the town was but a few minutes away.

Flat 4A would for the next nine months be home to three of Munterconnaught's more eccentric exports. The flat was as centrally located as the Rams could have hoped for, and was situated on the first floor of a reasonably large building, which was located close to a convenience shop and a night club. An art shop was located directly below the flat, and the owner, Mr. Conway, had arranged to meet Goosey there as soon as the boys arrived in Waterford. After reaching the shop with little difficulty, the boys paid a month's rent to Conway along with 150 pounds by way of deposit. Conway then introduced them to Rick Duffy who would act as rent collector, dropping by the flat each Tuesday to collect 25 pounds from each of the boys and a further 2 pounds to cover electricity expenses.

Rick was the spitting image of the ageing actor Mickey Rooney. He stood less than five foot tall and had a rather round face with a few well-groomed grey hairs at the back and sides of his head helping to complete the look. The Rams soon began referring to Rick as Mickey Rooney, and within weeks it would seem that everyone in Waterford knew of Mickey's doppelganger; everyone that is except for Rick himself.

Mickey accompanied the lads as they entered Flat 4A for the first time. As is often typical of student accommodation that has been lying empty for the summer months, given a bit of a cleaning and lightly brushed over with a tin of magnolia paint, first impressions of the flat weren't totally unfavourable.

The main door of the flat opened into one end of a u-shaped hall-way. The sitting room and small kitchen were located to the left of the entrance while two bedrooms and a bathroom were to be found at the other side of the flat. Some 'mod-cons', such as a kettle and run-ning water, were supplied. Others, namely a washing machine and tumble dryer, were stored upstairs and shared by all other tenants in the building.

With Mickey's grand tour complete, Rams and Goosey were free to take in the sights, which entailed finding the nearest off-licence, buying some alcohol and getting hammered. Both of the lads were lager drinkers but, almost in a bid to prove themselves as bonafide students, they opted for the cheaper delights of a bottle of wine each, which they made short work off back at the flat. Then it was time to check out a few of the local pubs until closing time. The next morn-ing they made a brief appearance at college to register and, later that evening, followed closely the drinking itinerary they had devised the previous day.

The following week would herald the beginning of college classes but this significant event would be overshadowed by the arrival of a certain Gavin O'Dowd.

Chapter 15

TURNING THE WATER INTO WINE

ANY FRESHER students initially perceive moving into a flat or house—away from the watchful eyes of their parents—to be one of the most exciting parts of going to college. But the euphoria often evaporates when the stark realisation of impending poverty looms.

Although Rams's parents financially assisted him whenever they could, he knew early on that these contributions wouldn't be sufficient to support him throughout college. Therefore, he obtained a 600 pounds overdraft from his bank and this, coupled with the meagre college grant, left him with a paltry weekly sum of 15 pounds to survive on after rent and bills were paid.

Goosey's financial woes almost equalled that of the Rams. But Dowd, upon arriving in Waterford a few days after the lads, quickly went about showing the pair how 15 pounds could be worth 100 if they followed his master course in economising. Dowd had spent the previous college year in Waterford so, second time round, he knew every trick in the book; hell, he probably wrote the book.

Despite Rams's initial misgivings, he and Dowd bonded almost immediately after they moved into Flat 4A and, in no time, the two were like thieves in the night, finding ever-inventive ways of furnishing the flat for free with the bare essentials, one of which was toilet roll.

Dowd had noticed, as you do, that the majority of public toilets at that time used the same type of toilet roll holders, but these were locked to deter any would-be thieves. He had discovered, however, that inserting an ordinary house key to the left of the simplistic locking mechanism and then turning it 90 degrees anti-clockwise would release the lock. The toilet roll could then be popped out of the holder and a quick twist of the key would lock the device again, making the burglary invisible to the naked eye; at least until some poor unfortunate would inevitably be caught short moments later while answering nature's call.

About every two months, Rams and Dowd would go on a 'toilet run' through the city centre. Most pubs in town stocked massive toilet rolls, each of which could cater for the arse-wiping needs of everyone in Flat 4A for three or four weeks. Therefore, these premises were the obvious targets for 'Operation Toilet Roll'.

'Operation Toilet Roll' always followed the same pre-determined plan. Both men, each carrying a newly-emptied school bag, would enter a pub that they were unlikely to frequent again. They would by-pass the bar and head straight to the toilets where one of them would 'work the safe' while his accomplice would stand at the urinal keeping an eye out for bar staff or anyone from *Crime Stoppers*. Once the goods were in the bag, the thieves would make haste to the next bar. Even though they weren't exactly robbing banks, the two lads got a tremendous buzz from escaping each bar without attracting any unwanted attention. On one occasion, however, they were nearly caught red-handed.

Rams and Dowd had knocked off two bars earlier in the evening and were pursuing one final toilet roll when they happened upon a pub they hadn't seen before. Upon entering the almost derelict premises, they spotted a sign for the toilets and didn't waste any time in following it.

While sauntering past the bar, Rams made eye contact with the barman but, undeterred by the dagger-like stare he received, he followed Dowd into the gents' toilets. Dowd disappeared into a cubicle in search of the Holy Grail while Rams stood at the urinal as if he was doing his business. He had barely taken position when the toilet door swung open, and in walked the barman. He took a brief look round the room and then placed himself at the opposite end of the trough-like urinal, a mere four feet away from the Rams.

Having used the toilet in the two previous bars, Rams didn't have anything left in the tank and the barman must also have recently emptied his bladder because he too stood at the urinal, feebly pretending to be dying for a piss but with not even the faintest sound of a trickle coming from his direction. From the corner of his eye, Rams could see the barman looking at him and he knew that he was on to him. By now, the silence in the toilets was unbearable, with the ever so slight yet obvious noise of Dowd tinkering with the toilet holder in the background adding to the tension.

As Dowd stepped out from the cubicle, a bulging schoolbag further evidence of his guilt, he nodded to the Rams and the pair quickly departed the building. It had been a close shave, but they had pulled it off, and hence their confidence grew and they continued to commit crimes against unsuspecting publicans. Indeed, as the months passed, the lads became so cocky that they would rob toilet roll and other small items at any given opportunity and from any premises they saw fit.

On one occasion, while enjoying a rare treat of a bag of chips in a deserted upstairs floor in Supermacs, Dowd asked Rams to go on a toilet run since he had a near-empty bag with him and there was nobody in sight. When Rams returned moments later, he was bemused to discover that Dowd had upstaged him by removing every light bulb from the first floor of the building and placing each of them calmly into his pockets, thereby ensuring that Flat 4A would be well lit up for the remainder of the college year.

Cablelink was another commodity that the lads could ill afford but couldn't do without either. For fear of dying from boredom in the flat, they had no choice but to rent a television from a nearby electrical shop. Yet, even with a set of rabbit's ears that Goosey had brought with him to Waterford, the lads could only muster the faintest reception from the television. A Cablelink connection would supply all the terrestrial stations and many more besides, but that came at a price and, having already splashed out on renting the television, the lads couldn't afford to pay cable bills.

Dowd surmised that all of the other residents in the building must surely have had a Cablelink connection, and so he decided to pay a visit to his closest neighbour who lived in a flat, which was situated further up the small flight of stairs that linked all the flats in the building together.

X-File Man, as he would come to be known, appeared to be a quiet yet mysterious character in his late forties who had been living in the area for many years. The lads had seen him coming and going but had not yet spoken to him, and Dowd was quite surprised, upon knocking on his door, to find a friendly albeit strange man welcoming him into his sitting room for a chat.

The first thing Dowd couldn't help but notice was that the walls of the flat were almost completely covered with posters and photographs of Gillian Anderson. She played the female lead character in *The X-Files*, which was one of the biggest shows on television at that time. A 12-year-old boy plastering his bedroom walls with posters of a television star is one thing, but when a middle-aged man does likewise with his entire living quarters, one could be forgiven for assuming that he needs to get out more often.

The plan was simple in theory. Dowd would ask X-File Man for permission to run a cable from his television to the one downstairs in Flat 4A. But one cannot simply cut to the chase on these occasions, and a bit of small talk was the least he could do by way of a common courtesy to his potential cable provider. Dowd was never a man short of a few words and, having exhausted the topic of how shite the weather had been for the past few weeks, he turned his attention to the posters adorning every wall in the room.

'I see you're a bit of a fan of Gillian there,' he remarked.

'Oh, she's an amazing woman,' answered X-File Man, his eyes lighting up at this rare opportunity to discuss his dream woman with a fellow human being.

'She's something special all right,' Dowd said, nodding his head and smiling as if trying to make himself believe what he was saying while simultaneously glancing at the door to ensure that it hadn't been locked behind him.

'There's Gillian eating an ice-cream,' returned X-File Man, pointing to a photo above the artificial fireplace. 'And there's one of her getting ready for bed.' An uncomfortable silence followed before he continued. 'That one over there is Gillian's sister. And beside that is a photo of Gillian brushing her teeth.'

Dowd was beginning to wish he'd raised the subject of the posters after asking about the cable. Meanwhile X-File Man continued ranting, his tongue now hanging out of his mouth, causing drool to slither menacingly down his chin.

Finally, as the Gillianophile caught his breath for a moment, an exasperated Dowd seized the opportunity and asked him about the cable. Fortunately, Dowd's tireless groundwork had put him into his neighbour's good books and, despite Dowd's half-hearted offer to contribute something towards his monthly Cablelink bill, X-File Man agreed to supply cable to the lads free of charge.

Later that day, Dowd and his flatmates visited a hardware shop with the view to buying a length of cable, which would be used to connect X-File Man's television to theirs, thereby providing them with the free cable Dowd had worked so hard to get.

'How much cable do you need?' asked the shopkeeper.

'About this much,' Dowd replied, throwing a ball of wool across the counter, to the bewilderment of the assistant.

Rather than risk guessing how much cable would be needed to connect the two flats, the lads had purchased a ball of wool and measured the distance, almost to the inch. Wool was cheap; cable was not and, if they'd haphazardly and incorrectly estimated that 40 feet of cable was needed when 30 feet would suffice, they would have been further out of pocket than necessary.

Returning to the flat with a cut-to-size piece of cable and connectors, the boys set to work in a scene that could have been straight out of *The A-Team*. Dowd, having briefly discussed the merits of Gillian Anderson's ample breasts with his neighbour, connected one end of the cable to X-File Man's television and then threw the remainder out the window to the Rams who was waiting below on a flat roof, which ran along the sitting room window of Flat 4A. He then passed the cable through the window to Goosey who, within seconds, hooked it into the back of the rented television.

Finally the lads had picture, sound and a means of entertainment. Nevertheless, the best entertainment is often self-created and that would ring true over the course of the following weeks and months in Flat 4A.

Chapter 16

NO PAIN, NO SHAME, NO BRAINS

WITH THE newly tuned-in television the only obvious antidote to unbearable boredom in Flat 4A, Rams and his flatmates were forced to stretch their imaginations if they were to succeed in finding alternative ways of entertaining themselves.

For Dowd, this often amounted to sitting on one of the armchairs and seeing how many farts he could squeeze out in a given period of time. In this regard, he hadn't changed a bit from the boy who, while in primary school, had frequently caused his fellow pupils to run a mile from him due to the over-powering effect of his all too regular emissions.

Occasionally the Rams would get into the spirit of things by accepting Dowd's challenge to partake in a farting competition. Goosey, none too impressed by this juvenile behaviour, would unwillingly act as referee but, in spite of his impartiality, many competitions would end indecisively in a double count out; or perhaps double blow-out is a more appropriate description.

When it came to farting in public, Dowd was completely beyond reproach. He knew his arse contained a small, rechargeable nuclear bomb of sorts, and he wasn't afraid to use this weapon on unsuspecting innocents. One Saturday night he and Rams went for a few pints in one of their favourite bars in Waterford. By the time they arrived, the place was reasonably busy, and there was no available seating in sight.

'I could do with a seat,' grumbled the Rams.

'Leave it to me,' replied Dowd, and before Rams had a chance to prevent his flatmate from dropping the big one, it was too late. Initially Rams didn't notice any smell whatsoever. Maybe he was just immune to Dowd's farts at this stage, or perhaps his sense of smell had been irreversibly damaged through months' of ceaseless farting competitions. Unfortunately, nobody else in the bar suffered from such medical conditions and, within seconds, several people began walking and then stampeding towards the other side of the bar.

Dowd turned to face the Rams, a smile spreading across his face that would put a Cheshire cat to shame. Although Rams was glad to get a seat, the dagger stares from the clientele across the room, coupled with an ongoing uncomfortable atmosphere, led him to correctly assume that he and Dowd would remain on their own in one half of the bar for the rest of the night.

Back in Flat 4A, the lads had realised that despite the abundance of free channels they were receiving on the television, there was seldom anything even remotely entertaining on. The Rams had taken it upon himself, amid moments of drunkenness, to stand on top of the television and jump up and down on it to protest against the rubbish that was being broadcast on each channel. The singer, Peter Andre, always seemed to be on MTV and his 'wretched' music would drive the Rams to despair, forcing him to momentarily cover the television with his jacket and press the mute button on the remote lest his eyes or ears be offended.

One day Dowd invited his college friend, Cha, over to the flat. Cha hadn't met Rams or Goosey previously so had no idea what to expect from his friend's flatmates. Upon walking into the sitting room, his eyes were immediately drawn towards a large jacket that was almost completely obscuring the television. On top of it, a rather animated individual was jumping up and down like a child on a bouncing castle. And across the room another chap, can of beer in hand, sat riveted to the television as if his favourite show was on.

'This is the Rams,' said Dowd to his friend, pointing at the demented Jack on the box. While saluting Cha, Rams lost his balance,

causing him and the television to go crashing onto the floor. He remained tangled amongst the coat, television and wires as Dowd introduced a speechless Cha to Goosey, whose eyes were still fixated
on the table where the television had been sitting. Cha left Flat 4A a
while later, shaking his head and wondering if he had just returned
from the *Twilight Zone*.

While Goosey certainly appeared to be the sanest and most sensible
of Flat 4A's residents, he was also the only one who showed any interest in keeping the place tidy. Dowd took great pride in leaving as big
a mess behind him as possible whereas the Rams, although relatively
tidy, wouldn't concern himself with general cleaning chores such as
Hoovering or cleaning the bathroom.

As well as keeping the flat reasonably clean, Goosey attempted
to brighten up the sitting room by sticking posters of sexy models
onto one of the walls. X-File Man even donated a photo of Gillian
Anderson to the cause, and Rams christened the newly-decorated area,
'The Wall of Shame'. Despite the dubious moniker, the posters were
all 'tasteful' so that they could be passed off as art rather than porn to
any would-be female visitors.

Goosey was also a dab hand in the kitchen and could rustle up
many types of meals. Rams—although a fussy eater at the best of
times—was rather partial to Goosey's patented Shepherd's pie. Every
Saturday the two lads would take a stroll down town in search of ingredients for a pie that would provide both of them with dinner for
two days.

Even though Rams had a food budget of almost zero, he loved visiting the supermarkets, where he would search out cheap deals that
would sustain him through the week. Items such as beans, bread and
chips formed a staple part of his diet, and water from the kitchen
tap quenched his thirst each day until the weekend when he'd treat
himself to one or two pints of milk. He and Goosey, due to their dif-
fering tastes in food, would carry separate baskets around the shop,
but would split the costs on some shared items. A packet of 10 choc-
ices was a weekly treat to which both of them would contribute the
princely sum of 40 pence.

Every so often the Rams would take something unusual or expensive from one of the shop shelves and stealthily place it in his unsuspecting flatmate's basket. He would then quickly pay for his shopping and wait a safe distance—but within view—from the till until Goosey took his turn to pay for his shopping. Occasionally Goosey would spot the suspect item prior to it being scanned by the shop assistant, and he'd attempt to remove it from his basket undetected. But, more often than not, the assistant would scan the item before Goosey could react and he'd then have to convince her that he'd changed his mind about purchasing a pair of rather fetching ladies' tights. He'd instantly realise that Rams was up to his old tricks again and would send an 'I'm going to fucking kill you' look in his direction.

Upon returning to the flat, it would be time to cook up a storm. Goosey normally took care of pretty much everything because one could probably have killed and skinned an actual shepherd in the time it would take the Rams to peel and slice a few vegetables. For his part, Rams took charge of supplying some oven chips to supplement the meal, and he also took on the added and pressurised responsibility of keeping an eye on the pie once it was in the oven.

Goosey once cooked a meal for Dowd whose insatiable appetite led the chef to believe that doing so again would be a waste of time. Goosey had been preparing a Chinese meal for himself and, since he had more than enough food to spare, asked Dowd if he wanted some dinner. Following a predictably resounding 'yes', Goosey cooked a large meal, which could have fed half of Africa. Both men cleared their plates and, such was the enormity of the portions, Goosey was visibly struggling to finish eating his. As the exhausted chef sat slumped in an armchair, unsure as to whether he'd ever be able to move again, Dowd rose from where he was sitting and headed to the kitchen.

'What's he up to now?' pondered Goosey.

'Right, it's time for dinner,' Dowd announced, and it became shockingly clear that his freshly-consumed meal had acted as nothing more than a starter.

Dowd then turned on the cooker and filled a wok full to the brim with rice, meat and vegetables, an entire jar of Uncle Ben's sauce rounding off the meal nicely. This was a typical dinner for the gourmand, and the show didn't stop there.

Dowd had stopped eating from dinner plates shortly after moving into Flat 4A. Plates just couldn't hold enough food, and there was never a clean one around when needed. Of course the lack of clean plates could be traced to Dowd himself who, upon finishing his dinner, would place the dirty plate along with the knife and fork under the cushion of the chair he was sitting on. He'd remain seated on the chair for the evening like a bird minding her eggs. Inevitably, the eggs would hatch some days later when Goosey would trace a putrid smell in the room to a blue-moulded plate covered with hair and bits of God knows what. The wok never suffered such a fate as it wouldn't fit under the armchair cushion and so it became Dowd's official dinner plate.

One evening Dowd was in the kitchen preparing dinner when Cha dropped round to the flat to say hello. Spotting the food-laden wok, he couldn't help but comment.

'That's a fair meal there, Gav. Do you cook for the boys every day?'

'No,' said Dowd, turning the cooker off and carrying the heavy wok to his armchair in the sitting room. 'This is just for me.'

Cha watched in amazement as Dowd tucked into the feed, using a huge wooden spoon in lieu of a knife and fork. This barbaric behaviour only cemented Cha's view that everyone in Flat 4A was barking mad.

Surprisingly, it often worked out almost as cheap to eat out than to go to the bother of cooking at home. The trick to this—as with everything else—was knowing where to find the bargains.

The Grapevine, which was the college's free weekly magazine, was issued on campus every Monday. Like many other college rags, its main use was in identifying where the best drinks promotions for the week would be held. But Goosey normally only picked up the magazine for one reason—Burger King vouchers. Each week a different 'Buy one, get one free' offer would feature in the magazine and, if it were of the Chicken Royale variety, Goosey would undoubtedly visit the fast food restaurant some evening that week.

A Chicken Royale meal included the chicken royale itself along with chips and a mineral. Burger King was usually half-empty whenever Goosey sat down to consume his two Chicken Royales, two bags of chips and two minerals. Therefore, he could pick a quiet corner in which to enjoy his meals in peace. One evening, much to Goosey's annoyance, the place was over-run by kids celebrating a birthday party. Almost a dozen of them surrounded his table, staring in awe and pointing at him while he devoured two trays of food. Unsurprisingly, Goosey chose the takeaway option thereafter but that little incident didn't deter him from making the most of any free offers that came his way.

A few weeks later Goosey arrived home from college with over 30 newspapers stuffed into his bag. He had been passing the students' union office when he spotted a stack of newspapers outside it with a 'free newspapers' sign hanging over them. Upon closer inspection, he noticed each newspaper carried a voucher for a free alcopop, which could be reclaimed at most bars in the country. Now Goosey wouldn't normally be caught dead drinking an alcopop but free drink is free drink and certainly, 'Beggars can't be choosers.'

Quickly checking that the coast was clear, Goosey put the sign into his pocket, packed every last one of the newspapers into his bag, and headed for home where he grabbed a scissors to carefully cut around each of the vouchers. He and Rams had been enduring an especially destitute week so they took extra delight in visiting a few pubs that night and having a free drink in each one of them before moving on. The following two evenings panned out in similar fashion until the well of free drink eventually ran dry.

If there was one thing almost as good as free drink, it was free food. Club L.A. was one of the biggest nightclubs in Waterford and one of Rams's favourite social haunts. Admission for students was free every Sunday night, and drinks promotions made certain that some beers and shots cost little to nothing, meaning that one could enjoy a few scoops without breaking the bank.

Dowd, as ever with one finger on the pulse, discovered that there was a little-known chipper located in the club, hidden through an archway just off the dance floor. Food was only served for a 30-minute period after midnight, but it was free to anyone possessing an admission stub for the club. The meal consisted of a very generous portion of sausages and chips, and it served as a lovely late night treat for the lads, especially if they'd been forced to stay in the flat all weekend due to financial constraints.

Even late at night, Dowd's appetite seldom waned and, having polished off his meal, he would leave the chipper and return moments later brandishing a new admission stub, which he'd have wrangled from the bouncer. He would then collect his second free meal and take a seat beside his flatmates, stabbing them with his fork if their hands came within an inch of his plate. Rams and Goosey seldom managed to pull off the same trick because the woman serving behind the counter would recognise them from moments earlier and would promptly refuse to serve them a second meal. If Dowd was recognised, however, he would turn on the charm and tell her, 'Ah, you must be confusing this beautiful face with somebody else.' Dowd's impromptu and cheeky responses never failed him, and he usually ended up with an extra large portion of food for his troubles.

Following several weeks of living together, it was obvious to Rams and Goosey that Dowd was somewhat lacking in the shame department and so, within time, Dowd received the nickname of 'No Shame'. Rams, not being privy to feeling much in the way of pain, became 'No Pain' and Goosey, despite often proving to be the most sensible in the flat, became 'No Brains'. For obvious reasons, he didn't particularly like his new nickname but learnt to take it with a pinch of salt.

Rams and Dowd even devised a catchphrase of sorts, which left visitors to the flat without any doubt as to who was who.

'I feel no pain,' the Rams would roar.

'I have no shame,' Dowd would say, and then he and Rams would point at Goosey, shouting in unison, 'and that man there has absolutely no brains.' Goosey, for his part, would look suitably unimpressed but couldn't help breaking a smile at the child-like carry-on of his two demented flatmates.

The catchphrase would be used for many years to come and in any part of the world that the three lads found themselves meeting up in. If nothing else, its origins served as a reminder to the lads of the borderline poverty days in Waterford that had brought the three of them closer together.

Chapter 17

NEW FACES FROM STRANGE PLACES

As with the move from primary to secondary school many years earlier, enrolling in college in September 1996 presented the Rams with an opportunity to make new friends. From the offset, the Multimedia course was split into three main groups, with Rams placed in one class and Goosey in another.

For the first time in his life, Rams became aware of his accent, the likes of which hadn't been heard before by some of his classmates, most of whom hailed from the south or south east of the country. Likewise, many of the accents of those same individuals were alien to the Rams—none more so than Trevor White's.

Trevor's strong Cork accent was impossible to mistake. But, as is indicative of youthful ignorance, he seemed to think that his accent was representative of every man in the country. Therefore, he considered Rams's strong Ulster dialect to be hilarious, and he had picked up on a few words that Rams pronounced differently to the southerners in the class.

'Say "book",' Trevor would demand, a broad smile stretching so far across his face that he was in danger of hurting himself. Rams's pronunciation of book rhymed with cook whereas everyone else's version rhymed with fuck. He pronounced other words—such as mirror and donkey—differently too, and was beginning to feel a touch paranoid until he realised that many of his fellow Cavan men spoke the exact same way.

Trevor laughed hysterically each time he perceived the Rams to mispronounce a word. Rams didn't mind though; he thought it ironic that the guy who found his accent so amusing came from a county where some people couldn't manage a single sentence without using one or all of the words 'langer', 'like' and 'boy'. Trevor was one such person.

Rams would exact good spirited revenge by taking the piss out of Trevor with his own exaggerated spin on the Cork accent.

'How are you doing boy? I was out last night, like, and the town was jointed, like. I was absolutely langers boy and the place was full of langers, like.'

Trevor would normally retaliate by asking Rams to repeat other words after him, and the banter between the two would continue in this way until the lecturer entered the classroom.

One guy who most people didn't dare tease was Winston Ralph. He was a Tipperary man who normally dressed in black and was an avid death metal fan. With around 30 students in the class, it wasn't surprising that a few weeks of the college year had passed before Winston and Rams exchanged words.

A roll call was taken each day during the 11.15 class, and Wednesday's Communications lesson occurred at this time. One day Rams and Winston were seated together, both of them bored shitless by the tiresome lesson that was in progress. The lecturer, a rather excitable woman in her thirties, could always be relied upon to churn out the same tired joke each time she happened upon Winston's name on the attendance sheet.

'Winston Ralph? Any relation to Winston Churchill?' she asked while appearing rather pleased with herself for coming up with this clever comparison for the umpteenth time.

'No,' was the rather blunt reply.

As the class continued, a discussion about stereotypes ensued, at which stage the lecturer challenged the class to give an example of, and a reason for, a particular stereotype.

Winston turned to face the Rams and ever so casually said, 'Black people; because they're black', and then carried on feigning interest in the serious topic of discussion that was taking place.

Now Rams was no racist but he also hated the political correctness that was beginning to engulf Irish society to such an extent that one could no longer refer to a minority of any sort without first checking in the dictionary to see that the latest correct term of description was being used. God forbid one might refer to somebody of short stature as anything other than vertically challenged. As such, Winston's old-fashioned sense of humour was a breath of fresh air and, within weeks, he and the Rams became good friends.

Early on in the college year, Rams also befriended a chap by the name of Scott Warner. He was a six foot-something Kerry man who, although very studious, had a similar sense of humour to the Rams. Like the residents of Flat 4A, Scott was a ridiculously poor student, living in digs during the week and sleeping on different friends' couches at weekends. Going home to Kerry for the weekend wasn't really an option as the trip involved a five-hour bus journey followed by a few miles of hitch-hiking, another bus trip and finally a short trip by car. Rams often joked that Scott needed to, 'take planes, trains and automobiles to get home'. Not wanting to suffer the delights of jet lag too often, Scott only went home at Christmas and Easter; so Waterford truly became his home for two years, whether he liked it or not.

The rest of the Multimedia students were a varied bunch, ranging in age from 17 to 33. Mature students were certainly an unknown quantity as far as the Rams was concerned, and it took him a while to adjust to their presence.

During the first week of college, Rams arrived late into a Mathematics lesson. The classroom was heaving with students and, as he entered the room, a woman in her early thirties swung round in her chair to face him. She was seated beside a student who she had appeared to be helping with a maths problem and, in his rushed state of mind, Rams forgot that the Mathematics lecturer was of the male variety.

'Sorry I'm late, Miss,' he said, taking his seat and turning a noticeable shade of red when the real lecturer entered the room seconds later and commenced the lesson.

Rams had always hung round with people within his age bracket and, despite being but 18 years of age, he soon realised that he could easily relate to those in the class who were several years older than him. Some of Goosey's new mates were also the wrong side of 21, including one lad who was a dead ringer for Jon Bon Jovi. In fact, Goosey only ever referred to him as Jon Bon Jovi, and many students, unaware of the traditional and unique christening customs in Munterconnaught, assumed that Jovi's doppelganger was indeed named after the famous rock legend.

Dowd's college class consisted of a smaller number of students so he had a select choice of friends, the maddest of whom was undoubtedly Paul Tritchler. Tritchy, as he was affectionately known, studied accountancy with Dowd, and occasionally dropped up to Flat 4A for a visit. He immediately became quite popular with Rams and Goosey due to his laidback and personable attitude and a sense of humour that was beyond compare. His many stories were always entertaining, thanks in no small part to their literal translations, which weren't always obvious in the first telling.

Tritchy might start a story by talking about the big drinking session he'd been on the previous night, how pissed he'd been and how the barman had thrown him out for dancing on the furniture.

'Well, I started shouting abuse at him,' he would say.

'And what exactly did you shout at him?' the Rams would innocently ask.

'Abuse, Abuse, Abuse,' would be the reply, and Tritchy would start shouting 'Abuse' for all he was worth while sounding like Father Jack Hackett after discovering a new word.

Dowd and Tritchy often went on the lash mid-week and would arrive back at the flat in the middle of the night, usually very drunk and carrying some sort of cumbersome souvenir from their drink-fuelled adventures. Rams and Goosey would awaken the next morning to see what presents the elves had left in the sitting room. A large stepladder, two empty beer kegs and a few county council cones were just some of the unwanted gifts discovered and then promptly dumped outside the flat by the two lads while Dowd and Tritchy were still sleeping.

With the flat looking somewhat respectable again, finding Tritchy would become the priority. The couch in Flat 4A was, if nothing else, reasonably comfortable and an adequate makeshift bed for anyone under the influence and in need of some shut-eye. But Tritchy always chose to sleep anywhere except on the couch and, on one occasion, Goosey awoke in the morning to find Tritchy fast asleep on top of the chest of drawers beside his bed. The piece of furniture was no more than four foot in length, meaning Tritchy had to bend his body into the shape of a boomerang just to fit into the confined space. Nonetheless, he awoke as if he had enjoyed the best night's sleep ever, hopped off the dresser and headed out the door to college with not a care in the world.

Tritchy worked part-time in his mother's flower shop from where he delivered bouquets throughout Waterford in the company van. Every few weeks he'd land into Flat 4A to collect Dowd, and the two would go on a drive, dropping into a few unknown pubs on the city's outskirts for a chat and a few drinks. An ever-empty wallet meant that Goosey seldom joined the lads and, although Rams was equally poor, he'd rustle up an emergency fiver so that he could accompany Dowd and Tritchy and get an opportunity to see parts of Waterford hitherto unvisited by him.

One February evening, following a few beverages in a quiet country pub just outside the city, the three lads returned to Flat 4A. Tritchy decided to stay the night, and the next morning he offered the Rams and Goosey a lift into college. The two lads were appreciative of the offer as they were booked onto a class trip to Intel that morning and the bus was due to leave the college at 9 o'clock sharp. Tritchy's van would get them there a good deal quicker than the 30-minute walk they were accustomed to.

As Tritchy drove along the quays, the morning traffic was rather busy but moving smoothly nonetheless. Goosey was seated at the back of the van, his eyes still half-closed from having to get up at such an ungodly hour. Rams was positioned in the passenger's seat beside Tritchy who was joking and messing as usual.

'So what will ya be singing on the bus today, Rams?' he asked, before attempting to answer the question himself. *'The wheels on the bus go round and round,* maybe?'

'That's the one all right,' laughed the Rams, and with that Tritchy burst into song, loudly tapping the steering wheel while nudging the Rams as if encouraging him to join in.

'The wheels on the bus go round and round,
Round and round, round and round,
The wheels on the bus go round and round,
All through the town.'

As Tritchy's singing continued, Rams noticed the large bus ahead of them was coming to a halt in front of the traffic lights, which had just turned red. Although he tried to say something, the words wouldn't come fast enough, and he was forced to watch in silence as the bus appeared to get closer and closer. Meanwhile Tritchy was singing louder and more enthusiastically than before, and he looked as if he might explode at any minute.

'The wheels on the bus go round and round,
Round and round, round and rou...'

Tritchy came back to Earth with a loud thud as his van crashed into the back of the bus; the irony of the situation becoming shockingly apparent now that the wheels on this very real bus were no longer going round and round. Fortunately, Tritchy had been driving quite slowly so all three of the lads escaped from the vehicle injury-free. But the same could not be said for the van, which suffered significant dents to the front bonnet. With only a few minutes remaining until the bus bound for Intel was due to leave the college grounds, Rams and Goosey were forced to bid Tritchy farewell, leaving him in the unenviable position of having to explain to the bus driver how he managed to drive into the rear end of the bus. The Rams reckoned any story Tritchy could conjure up would be more believable than the truth.

The lads didn't see sight or sound of Tritchy for about a month after the bus incident, and then one evening he dropped into Flat 4A unannounced. As ever, he was in great form and revealed that he was driving a brand new van. Following several minutes' small talk, he asked the lads if they wanted to go for a drink in Tramore, a seaside town situated outside Waterford city. Goosey declined the offer but Rams and Dowd, ever the parched camels, didn't need to be asked a second time.

Tritchy jokingly banished the Rams to the back of the van, labelling him a jinx for causing the crash and destroying his previous van a few weeks earlier. He then offered Dowd the honourable position of sitting in the passenger seat beside him.

As the van neared Tramore, the engine started rattling a little so Tritchy pulled over to the side of the road and popped open the bonnet to inspect the noise. Not finding anything untoward, he hopped back into the vehicle, and drove towards Tramore where he and the lads enjoyed a few drinks, with a bag of chips rounding off an enjoyable evening.

It was a pitch-dark night as the lads made the journey home. Tritchy was joking about how he'd never sing 'that fucking bus song' again when suddenly there was a startling bang and a massive object hit the front windscreen of the van. Tritchy couldn't see a thing but managed to brake quickly, bringing the van to a standstill. As the three lads emerged from the vehicle, the van's headlights made it possible for them to see that the bonnet had swung open and almost completely covered the windscreen. Miraculously the glass didn't break or crack, but the bonnet itself was bent right out of shape, and it took several minutes of banging and pushing before it could be forced into its original closed position.

Tritchy instantly realised that he mustn't have properly closed the bonnet when he inspected the engine earlier that night, and the near catastrophic accident had been a ticking time bomb. That stark realisation, however, didn't prevent him from turning round to the Rams with a cheeky grin on his face while declaring, 'Rams, you're a fuckin' jinx.' And, to be fair, perhaps he had a point.

Chapter 18

THE FALL OF THE HOUSE OF MUNCHIES

A FRIENDSHIP BETWEEN two people is something that requires time and effort from both parties. It's a bit like building a house. A good foundation is an essential starting point and, with that complete, the house can be slowly built up from the ground, brick by brick. Nevertheless, some people make the mistake of assuming that just because the building work has been completed, the house will stand for years to come. This is not the case, and any house neglected for too long will eventually crumble, whereas one that is maintained to a reasonable standard will stand the test of time.

When the Rams moved his whole life from Cavan down to Waterford in 1996, he left behind several such metaphorical houses, none of which he was prepared to let fall by the wayside. Unfortunately, keeping in contact with family and friends at home wasn't always easy. It would be four years before Rams would own his first mobile phone, and most of his friends didn't have or know how to use email. Therefore, the only viable method of communication available to him was via the use of public pay phones.

Having been short-listed for a 'Poorest Student of the Year' award, Rams could ill afford to spend much money on phone calls. Fortunately, the irrepressible man with no shame had discovered that it was possible to avail of free calls at a certain hotel along the quays. All one had to do was key a certain numeric code into the pay phone, dial the required phone number and—hey presto—free connection. The phone was located in the hotel lobby, but it was within view of the reception so the lads made sure never to outstay their welcome. Dowd would visit each Saturday evening to call home while Rams and Goosey would do likewise the following night. This system served them well for many weeks until eventually the code wouldn't work, and it appeared that their scam had been discovered.

Once again the Rams was forced to rely on his own diminutive funds to make ever so short calls from a pay phone on the street. He would always ring his parents to ensure all was well at home, and he'd then call one or two of his friends for a quick chat about the latest goings on in and around Oldcastle.

So as not to lose touch with the remainder of his friends at home, Rams religiously returned to Virginia for a weekend every third week, at which time his parents would give him a few pounds—equating to 15 pounds per week—to help him survive until his next visit. They'd also subsidise his social kitty for that weekend, allowing him to meet up with all the lads in Oldcastle for a night on the town.

There was something reassuring for the Rams about arriving in a pub in Oldcastle to find each of his friends sitting at the usual spot at the bar and enjoying the conversation and craic that had for years been synonymous with a good night out in the town. After numerous pints, the boys would take a mini-bus to the Springs and, with the bus speeding through the quiet country roads, Rams could always be heard singing boisterous songs while the lads would join in for the chorus.

Back in Waterford, the end of the college year was approaching and Dowd was still surprising Rams and Goosey with his ingenious ways of saving money. There was no washing machine or dryer in Flat 4A. Both such necessities were located in a communal room on the top floor of the building. A meter provided power to the machines, and it only cost an average of a pound to fund a full wash and dry. But why pay a pound for something that you can get for free? That was Dowd's ethos.

The shameless one would always wait until the weekend before deciding to do his laundry, since that peak period virtually guaranteed that the washing machine and dryer would be occupied. Upon arriving upstairs, Dowd would empty the contents of the washing machine mid-cycle, place his own clothes inside, reset the machine and return to the flat to make his dinner. He'd casually revisit the laundry room within minutes of his wash finishing, at which time he'd place his clothes in the dryer and shove the damp clothes, which he had displaced some time earlier, back into the washing machine. Dowd's impeccably-timed departure from the crime scene usually coincided with the money in the meter running out, thereby depriving the room of electricity. Some time later, the owner of the still damp and dirty laundry would make an appearance and, assuming that the meter had devoured the money, he would top it up with another pound coin. Since the same meter powered both washer and dryer, Dowd's clothes were always dried for free and often folded up neatly on top of the dryer when he'd collect them the following morning.

As the months passed by in Flat 4A, Rams and Dowd were acting more juvenile than ever before. The farting competitions had become something of a tired formula so one day, while a disinterested Goosey watched television rather than refereeing a match, Dowd appeared out of nowhere and unleashed the mother of all farts in front of the referee's face. In doing so, his arse made a noise, which suggested that more than just wind had been released, and an enraged Goosey indicated as much when he stood up and roared, 'There was liquid involved in that.' Rams and Dowd ached in laughter at Goosey's impromptu remark, and so a new catchphrase was born; one that would be used every time Dowd dropped a dead animal into his trousers.

By now, Flat 4A had garnered a reputation around college for being the biggest shit hole any student had ever lived in. Slowly the flat was beginning to fall apart; Rams, Dowd and indeed Tritchy only too eager to help it on its way.

One night an intoxicated Rams and Tritchy were attempting to outwrestle each other in the hallway. Tritchy charged towards the Rams, who managed to sidestep the attack at the last moment, but the aggressor's boot continued onwards and went crashing through the plasterboard wall. The resulting hole was as wide as a child's head and, after gaping into the hole, it became apparent that fixing the damage would be no mean feat because a distance of at least 30 centimetres stood between the plasterboard and the outer brick wall of the building. Fortunately, Goosey was at hand to bail the lads out, and the next day he miraculously managed to prop up the inside of the plasterboard using a few empty beer cans. A bit of filler and a dab of magnolia paint later and the 'hole in the wall machine'—as Rams and Dowd referred to it—was no more.

With the end-of-year college exams fast approaching, Rams and Dowd decided to visit the library one evening to attempt some well overdue studying. For once, Goosey was surely guaranteed a peaceful evening with nobody farting in his face or knocking in walls.

Upon arriving at the library, the two lads sat facing each other at a table upstairs. The deafening silence of the library created an ideal atmosphere for quality study but, after an arduous five minutes' reading, Dowd's concentration broke and, grabbing Rams's pencil case, he threw it over the balcony railing, which overlooked the ground floor of the library.

Rams was furious, but the laws of the library dictated that he keep all expletives issued to Dowd no louder than a whisper. He raced downstairs and, just as he picked up his pencil case, a torrent of his notes and belongings flew over the railing, clattering him on the head. Picking everything up, he went upstairs with the intention of throwing Dowd's pens and notes over the railing. But Dowd had packed them into his bag and, as the two lads sat quietly staring at each other with no notes on the table, it became obvious that no more studying would be done that evening. Therefore, they called a truce and decided to go home.

On the way home Dowd spotted an empty shopping trolley and he beckoned the Rams to hop into it. Rams duly obliged and, once onboard, No Shame slowly began pushing the trolley up the street. Then, picking up speed, he broke into a jog until eventually he was sprinting through the city centre with the trolley and excitable passenger in tow. Five minutes later Goosey was mildly surprised, upon returning from the bathroom to the sitting room, to find Rams and Dowd jumping up and down in a shopping trolley.

'I see yas are done studying for the evening,' he remarked, before taking his seat in front of the television. As Dowd recounted the events of the evening to a disinterested Goosey, Rams attempted to steer the trolley around the flat while simultaneously standing in it. As he departed the sitting room and rounded the first corner in the hallway, Goosey's prophetic voice could be heard in the background.

'Mind the walls, you fuckin' eejit.'

'They'll be all right,' Rams retorted, and five seconds later a loud bang suggested that perhaps they wouldn't be.

The collision with the wall had caused a large section of plaster and stone to fall onto the floor. Fortunately, Goosey still had plenty of filler and paint left over from the recent renovations, and once again he ensured that, despite Rams's needless trail of wanton destruction, the flat would remain standing for another day.

Having witnessed first-hand Rams's disregard for all property, Goosey should have realised that no part of the flat was safe from him if he went on the warpath. One day, amid a moment of boredom, Goosey purposely clipped his flatmate across the head and then ran through the hallway to avoid the imminent retaliation he knew was coming. Rams gave chase but Goosey managed to safely reach the bathroom, slamming the door shut behind him. Nevertheless, Rams continued his run and, upon reaching the door, he drew a big size 10 boot at it, knocking it completely off its hinges and out of the wooden frame from where it had hung for many years. Goosey caught the door as it flew across the small bathroom towards him and, for once, he looked aghast at Rams's actions.

Although the door itself remained largely undamaged, the hinges were destroyed and would need replacing before the door could be re-attached to the frame. With no money to spare for new hinges, Rams grabbed the shoddy excuse for a door and positioned it against a wall in the hallway where it remained for several weeks. By the time three girls from college came visiting a month later, the residents of Flat 4A were perfectly at ease with having a door-free bathroom. The girls lived a short distance away, and dropped into the flat every now and again to say hello. Twenty minutes after arriving, Rita—the oldest of the girls—excused herself from the sitting room. She returned seconds later looking rather perplexed.

'What's up, Rita?' asked the Rams.

'Eh, the bathroom door is in the hallway,' she replied meekly.

'Jaysis, how did it get there? Sure, follow me and I'll sort this out.'

Rams led Rita towards the bathroom and, once outside it, he signalled her to step into the room, which she did albeit somewhat sheepishly. Picking up the door, Rams placed it into the wooden frame and then returned to the sitting room.

'Let a roar up the hallway when you're done and I'll let you out,' he shouted through the door before leaving.

On subsequent visits Rita refused to make use of the bathroom even though the door had been permanently returned to its rightful place a few days after her embarrassing episode. As one might imagine, it was Goosey who once again mended the dilapidated flat and prevented it from caving in on him and his reckless flatmates.

At least Goosey could look forward to the end of the college year, and this would surely present him with the opportunity to finally escape Flat 4A for good.

Chapter 19

HIDE AND SEEK

THREE WEEKS before the end of the college year, Dowd came up with one of his most ingenious and devious money-saving schemes yet.

Mickey Rooney collected the rent at Flat 4A every Tuesday evening. Each of the lads would pay their rent in cash to him, and he would then write his initials into their respective rent books to indicate that he had received the payment. Because the rent collection was based on individual contributions rather than one large payment, Dowd reckoned if he was to tell Mickey that he was finishing college a few weeks earlier than planned and would be moving out of the flat, there was a chance Mickey would allow Rams and Goosey to remain as tenants while making the same individual rent payments as before. The degenerative state of the flat indicated that it would definitely lie idle for the summer months, so surely Mickey wouldn't risk Rams and Goosey moving out three weeks early, which could happen if he was to ask them to pay more rent in Dowd's absence.

As predicted by the man severely lacking in shame, Mickey took the bait and told the lads that Dowd could move out and the remaining pair could continue paying 27 pounds each a week in rent for the final three weeks of the college year.

Of course Dowd never moved out. Instead, he threw all of his belongings into the wardrobe in his room and, when going down town, ineptly disguised himself by wearing a baseball cap. Mickey lived on the same street as the lads so the chances of meeting him while sneaking about were quite high. Nevertheless, two weeks passed and, despite a few close shaves, Dowd's disguise did the trick, and he continued to live in Flat 4A rent-free and undetected by the rent collector. With his luck riding high, he encouraged Goosey to tell Mickey that he too had also finished his exams and would be leaving the flat and Waterford a week earlier than planned. Mickey said it wasn't a problem, gave Goosey back his deposit, and subsequently allowed the Rams to remain in the flat for the final week of the exams while paying just 27 pounds in rent.

As a result of Mickey's generosity, Goosey and Dowd had saved 108 pounds between them, but it was agreed that the money would be split evenly between all three lads. After all, Rams was now the only legitimate tenant in the flat, thereby ensuring that he would have to take the heat should Mickey suspect that two Munterconnaught refugees were holed up in Flat 4A. Each man's share worked out at 36 pounds. This might not have seemed like a lot of money to most people, but it was a small fortune to the lads and would go some way towards ensuring they enjoyed the remaining days of the term.

The final day of the exams eventually arrived, bringing with it the promise of a drinking session from hell. Rams and Goosey left the exam hall in jubilant spirits and, in no time, were drinking pints in the student bar with Winston, Scott and several other classmates. Stephen Gammell, who had arrived in Waterford the previous night, was also present along with Dowd and a few of his friends. Eventually Rams, Goosey, Dowd and Gammell decided to continue the drinking in Flat 4A where some homemade vodka and wine were awaiting them.

A tiny brewery was located just a few minutes' walk from Flat 4A. Its location was unknown to many people, but within its sacred walls one could buy bottles of wine and vodka and—for those feeling a bit adventurous—beer-brewing equipment and ingredients. Rams and Goosey had stumbled upon the brewery one day while out walking, and became loyal customers thereafter. A bottle of vodka cost a paltry five pounds while red wine, which was sold by the gallon, was 13 pounds.

The Rams always purchased the vodka, but Goosey preferred the wine, which contained enough alcohol to knock out a horse. More often than not, Goosey alone drank the entire gallon and miraculously still had a thirst for beer afterwards. Only one of his college friends ever managed to cover himself in glory by drinking half a gallon of the stuff, and everyone else who attempted to knock back this demon of a drink became shockingly drunk on the slightest amount.

Andy Rooney was an easy-going Dubliner who was in the same class as the Rams. One evening, prior to heading out for the night, Andy was amongst a small group of students who were drinking in Flat 4A. Goosey poured a pint of the infamous red wine and handed it to him.

'Ah, I won't drink all that, Goosey,' said Andy, looking somewhat apprehensive.

'Get it into ya, Horse,' replied Goosey, before pouring a large glass for himself.

Andy began sipping the wine but, within 20 minutes and with only a quarter of the glass drank, he turned an ungodly shade of green and passed out in the armchair he had been sitting on. The lads tried in vain to wake him but—not wanting to see a great night wasted—they went to a night club shortly thereafter, leaving Rooney slumped in the armchair looking like a miniature version of the Incredible Hulk.

Viv Duignan was another student who fell victim to the red wine, albeit without the same pigment-altering repercussions that Andy had endured. On the night of a class party, Viv drank a small amount of the brew in Flat 4A, and then later took into a feed of drink at the party. He returned to the flat that night and slept on the couch, apparently no worse off than if he had only been drinking beer for the evening.

The Rams awoke early the next morning. He and Goosey shared a bedroom and such were the cramped conditions of the room that a distance of only two feet separated the two parallel beds. Just as he was about to rise from the almost-warm sanctuary of his bed, Rams spotted a few bits of what appeared to be vomit stuck to the outer top side of his duvet. A glance to the floor confirmed his fears. Looking up at him was a large, perfectly circular, hard lump of vomit, which was stuck to the carpet in the dead centre of the small piece of floor separating the two beds.

Excessive drinking rarely made the Rams sick, and such a misfortune had never befallen him while sleeping. Looking over at Goosey's bed, he spotted a few dollops of vomit on his duvet too. Rams had never known Goosey to regurgitate except when he purposely did so as a party-piece from time to time while in secondary school. But on this occasion, a mountain of evidence was literally piled up on the floor, so Rams shouted over to the suspect in an attempt to wake him and get some answers. Goosey woke with a start and Rams pointed to the decorative ornament dividing them. Goosey was adamant that he was innocent and, after several minutes of blaming each other for the mess, two light bulbs suddenly lit up simultaneously above the lads' heads, and they gasped aloud.

'Viv.'

Viv was nowhere to be seen when the lads burst into the sitting room. He had already left for college, but Dowd was able to confirm that a very inebriated Viv had entered his room the previous night looking for the bathroom. Dowd had directed him to the room next door, but the lump of vomit in the lads' bedroom suggested that Viv had taken a left when he should have taken a right.

Even when nobody was drinking it, the homemade wine created a fair share of problems. A few months earlier, Goosey brought a gallon of it home with him to Cavan where he planned on presenting it to his parents as a Christmas gift. En route, he decided to stop in Dublin for an hour's shopping and, not wanting to lug a heavy container around with him, carefully placed the wine into a sports bag and pushed it under a bench in a city centre shopping centre. The bag was quite small and had to be forced closed so that it ended up resembling a beer keg with polyester handles.

Upon returning to the bench a short while later, Goosey was somewhat surprised to discover that the precious gift was missing. As he frantically combed the area, he noticed two security men in the distance walking away with the bag. Darting across the shopping centre, he was forced to spend five minutes convincing them that the 'suspect device' was in fact a very large bottle of wine and that he wasn't or never had been part of a paramilitary organisation.

Back in Waterford, amid the euphoria surrounding the end-of-year exams, a farrago of drink filled every corner of Flat 4A. The home-made wine and vodka were in abundance, along with various canned beers, and the noise emanating from the flat must have been signifi-cant by the time a knock came on the door. Although each of the lads were quite drunk, they were sober enough to realise that this unan-nounced visitor could be but one person—Mickey Rooney.

Goosey and Dowd ran for cover, and the Rams opened the door to Mickey who, after stepping into the sitting room, seemed rather sur-prised that Rams and Gammell were the only people present. Just sec-onds earlier it sounded like hundreds of people were partying on the premises, and now there was barely a sinner about. Somewhat flus-tered, Mickey began making arrangements to return Rams's deposit for the flat. But before that could happen, he needed to have a brief look around to ensure that the accommodation was still in the same state of disrepair that it had been at the beginning of the college year.

Rams followed Mickey towards Dowd's bedroom where, unbe-knownst to either of them, Goosey was hiding in the wardrobe, using one hand to hold the doors shut and the other to cover his nose so as to avoid inhaling the fumes from the abomination beside him that was Dowd's underwear hamper.

Fortunately, at a casual glance the room appeared not to have been lived in for several weeks. The bed was bereft of linen, and an open window ensured that some level of ventilation had helped neutralise any remaining Dowd odours.

'Yon lad just has to collect a few clothes from the wardrobe there, if you want to have a look,' said the Rams, unaware that Goosey was by now clinging for dear life to the insides of the wardrobe doors lest Mickey try to prise them open.

'No, that's all right. Everything seems fine here,' said Mickey, before asking to see the other rooms. The tour continued until the pair ended up in the kitchen. Rams was the first to enter the tiny room where he immediately spotted all six foot two inches of Gavin O'Dowd standing behind the kitchen door. With the grace of a ninja, Rams repositioned himself in front of the small gap between the door and wall where Dowd was doing a poor Anne Frank impression. Since Mickey was over a foot smaller than the Rams, there was little chance of him catching a glance of the shadowy figure over Rams's shoulder. But Rams was taking no chances and attempted to appear even taller by standing on his tippytoes and placing his hands on his head while looking down at the ever-shrinking Mickey.

Eventually Mickey wrapped up the conversation. His unannounced tour of the flat had been fruitless and, much to the relief of the Rams and his camouflaged flatmates, the suspicious rent-collector said his goodbyes and made for the door. Almost immediately, the boisterous banter and celebrations resumed in Flat 4A, continuing into the night across numerous watering holes in the city.

The following morning Rams and Goosey made the long, tiresome bus journey to Cavan. Dowd, on the other hand, decided to stay another night in the flat so that he could bid farewell to a few friends. He had completed his accountancy course in Waterford and, having decided to pursue his career in London, knew that it might be some time before he'd see some of his friends again.

Dowd's final task in Flat 4A was to return the rented television to the shop from whence it came. Unfortunately, Rams's weekly *Riverdance* performances had taken their toll on the set so, after due consideration, Dowd opted to leave it in the flat rather than face the wrath of the shop manager who would undoubtedly want to know why the television now resembled something that had been pushed through a letterbox.

As he closed the door to Flat 4A for the final time, Dowd reflected on what had been the most surreal year of his life. He certainly wouldn't miss the poverty that had befallen him in Waterford, but a part of him already longed to return there in the autumn with Rams and Goosey for what would inevitably be another unforgettable year.

Chapter 20

THE HEIGHT OF STUPIDITY, THE DEPTHS OF DESPAIR

Dowd wasn't the only London-bound Munterconnaught man in the summer of 1997. Goosey's brother, Peter, had lived in the city for some time and, since there was a vacant bedroom in his place, Goosey decided to spend the college break in the company of her majesty's subjects, earning a few pounds by digging holes and laying pipes underground on the London subway.

As September approached—and with it the beginning of a new college year—Goosey contacted the Rams with regards to securing accommodation in Waterford prior to the commencement of the first term. Since Goosey would be in London right up until the first week in September, it would be up to the Rams to travel from Cavan to Waterford in search of suitable accommodation.

'I don't care what kind of a place you get once it's not Flat 4A. Just don't get Flat 4A,' Goosey pleaded before hanging up the phone.

Rams also had a summer job, but it didn't pay too well. Therefore, he couldn't afford to take more than one unpaid day's leave. This meant entertaining the unimaginably torturous idea of travelling by bus to Waterford and returning to Cavan on the same day. This would encompass over 10 hours' travelling, which was testament to the third-world infrastructure and public transport that Irish people were forced to endure.

Arriving in Waterford, the Rams had a little less than two hours to find a home. With the internet still in its infancy, the only way he could hope to spot anywhere remotely suitable would be from combing through the morning's newspapers. Unfortunately, a few phone calls confirmed that most decent dwellings had been snapped up a few hours prior to his late-afternoon arrival in the city. At last, however, he happened upon an advertisement for a three-bedroom house, centrally located and within a few hundred yards from the phone box where he was standing. .

'*This looks promising,*' he thought, dialling the number included with the advert. A gentleman, who identified himself as an auctioneer named Joe, agreed to immediately meet the Rams on a city centre street.

Ten minutes passed by and the Rams was still waiting patiently for Joe to arrive. For the majority of that time a suited businessman had been leaning against a railing a few feet away, occasionally glancing over in Rams's direction. Realising that time was against him, the Rams called out to the stranger, the returned greeting leaving him in no doubt that he was now speaking to the auctioneer. Joe seemed almost surprised that Rams was the same person he had conversed with over the phone, but the confused expression quickly gave way to one of cheer, and he spoke amicably with the Rams as the pair walked the short distance to a house around which Joe provided Rams with a grand tour before sitting down to talk business.

The house was nothing special, but it goes without saying that it was a definite improvement on Flat 4A. It had three reasonably sized bedrooms and its location was quite close to the part of the city the Rams was most accustomed to. Having asked the usual pre-rental questions regarding bills and utilities, Rams put the million-dollar question to the auctioneer.

'So how much is this place per month?' he asked.

'It works out at 32 pounds each per week,' replied Joe, alluding to Rams's earlier comment that he would be moving two other people in with him. The rent was a little higher than Rams had hoped for but, with only 20 minutes remaining until the bus for Dublin departed, this was not the time to be playing hardball.

'Well, I'd be fairly interested in taking the place. How much of a deposit are you looking for?'

'Five percent of the value of the house and, once I receive that, I can hold the place if you're waiting for your mortgage to be processed.'

'What was that?' gasped the Rams, scarcely comprehending what he was hearing and almost needing to hear it repeated lest his ears were deceiving him. 'You said something about a mortgage there. Is this place not for renting?' he asked.

'Of course not,' Joe replied, looking slightly peeved upon realising that he had wasted valuable time showboating the house to the poorest student in Ireland. 'I was thinking you were a bit young to be buying the place,' he added, before quickly showing Rams the door.

With mere moments remaining until the call of Cavan beckoned, Rams sprinted to a nearby phone box from where he dialled Mickey Rooney's mobile number. It was the last thing he wanted to do but, given the circumstances, he didn't see himself as having much of a choice.

Mickey's phone rang for several seconds before an unmistakable gruff voice could be heard at the other end of the line. Rams rushed through the necessary small talk before asking if Mr. Conway had any properties other than Flat 4A available for renting at that time. Apparently Conway had a nice vacant town house, which would be perfect for the lads. But since Mickey was attending a horse racing event in Tramore that day and Rams was rushing back to Cavan, it was agreed that Rams would ring Mickey the following day to continue the conversation and perhaps—at least in Rams's mind—provisionally agree to rent the property.

Unfortunately, the resultant telephone call squashed any hopes Rams had of living in anything other than squalor for the college year. Mickey, changing his story from the previous day, stated that the house was undergoing refurbishment and wouldn't be ready before Christmas. All was not lost, however, because another property was available for renting immediately and at a fair price.

'Goosey, how's it going?' yelled the Rams into the telephone receiver.

'Not too bad. How did ya get on in Waterford?'

'I have good news and I have bad news.'

'What do you mean, Rams?' asked Goosey, sounding slightly concerned.

'The good news is that I found us a place to live in for the year.'

'Nice one; for a minute there I thought you were going to say you got nothing.'

'Well, the bad news is that it's Flat 4A.'

And with that, the phone went dead.

Despite Rams's best intentions, he had lumbered himself and Goosey with Flat 4A for a second consecutive year. Fortunately, Goosey calmed down before he returned from London, by which time Winston had agreed to move into the flat with the lads, thereby ensuring the vacuum created by Dowd's absence would be adequately filled. A coin toss presented Goosey with Dowd's old room, hence a tiny silver lining amidst the rather large cloud that was hovering over his head.

As was typical of young Irish people, the return to college meant one thing to Rams and his flatmates: a monumental piss-up. Having already come close to accidentally purchasing a house, Rams was on a roll when it came to making moronic mistakes that defied belief. Therefore, during the first week back at college, he convinced Goosey and Winston that it was Freshers' week and hence the biggest social occasion of the year before Christmas.

With only a handful of classes timetabled for the remainder of the week, the trio decided to avoid college for those days, and instead went on the lash, drinking late every night and sleeping during the day. The town's pubs, however, were only half-full each night, which was incomprehensible considering the social magnitude of Freshers' week. Following three nights of this sedate, albeit expensive drinking, the lads were at home discussing the graveness of the situation when a knock on the door interrupted the debate.

The ineluctable Mickey Rooney entered the flat. It wasn't his first time visiting that week, or even his second or third for that matter. In fact, this was the fourth time—in as many days—in which Mickey had come knocking on the door unannounced. On each occasion the lads were drinking cans of cheap lager, and the associated noise emanating from the flat must have attracted Mickey's attention. He collected the rent on his initial visit and this was a genuine reason for dropping over. But the following day he sauntered through the open door of Flat 4A for no reason other than to check with the lads that everything was working okay in the flat. By the time of his third visit, Mickey's excuses for dropping by were rather dubious, to say the least.

'Could I borrow a pen for a few minutes, lads?'

And by day four, the lads were beginning to wonder if Mickey was smoking more than just tobacco in his pipe.

'Do any of you boys own the green car that's parked out on the street?' he asked; his tone of voice implying that his query was genuine, but Rams suspected otherwise.

On each of Mickey's previous visits, he had commented—somewhat light-heartedly—on the drinking that was taking place in the flat.

'You're having a few drinks, lads?'

And now on Mickey's final visit of the week, it almost seemed that he was pissed off because the lads appeared to be partying every evening.

'Drinking again, lads?' he said while glancing around the room, which was covered with empty beer cans.

'We are indeed. Will ya join us for one?' asked the Rams jokingly.

'I'll not, thanks,' Mickey replied, and walked towards the door. Suddenly, he turned around and delivered a parting shot.

'By the way lads; the rent will be going up to 33 pounds from next week to cover the electricity bills.'

The three flatmates agreed to the increase, but as soon as Mickey departed the scene, a new debate began—this time on the subject of Mickey Rooney and what the hell he was up to. He had already increased the rent by three pounds from the previous year and, now just a few days after moving in, he was attempting to up the rent again by the same amount. Rams was having none of it.

'He's acting the bollocks, boys. He's obviously seen us drinking here every evening and thinks we must be loaded with cash, so he has decided to put up the rent—without Conway knowing—and he'll pocket the extra money himself. It's obvious he's been dropping up here all week just so he could suss us out.'

Goosey felt there might be some substance to Rams's theory, so the following day the two lads landed on Mickey's doorstep to put the theory to the test.

'How's it going? We discussed the rent increase last night and we just don't think we can afford to pay that much, so I think we'll have to move ou...' Goosey's heart-breaking spiel was interrupted mid-flow.

'It's okay lads. I had a word with Mr. Conway this morning and I told him the increase was a bit much, so he has agreed to leave things the way they are.'

The lads had cleverly called Mickey's bluff and, as expected, he immediately backtracked in an attempt to paint himself as some sort of good-will Samaritan who had stood up to Mr. Conway. Mickey had made the mistake of presuming the lads were rich, but they knew better than anyone that this was not the case, and they wouldn't have to wait long for this fact to come to the fore.

The following Monday the Flat 4A trio returned to college, only to discover that Freshers' week had just commenced. Having celebrated the occasion a week earlier, Rams and Winston cursed their bad luck at having no money left in the kitty to fund another week-long drinking spree.

Unlike his flatmates, who had little to show after a summer's work, Goosey had returned to Ireland with two thousand pounds in his pocket. Considering how strapped for cash he had been during the previous college year, he might as well have won the lottery. He decided, however, to refrain from excessive spending during Freshers' week because his newfound wealth would, if managed correctly, allow him to live in relative comfort for the remainder of the college year. Unfortunately, despite his good intentions, Goosey soon began spending money as if he had indeed scooped a lottery jackpot.

As per the previous year, obtaining a television became a priority

for the lads once the initial week's partying was over. The cable from
X-File Man's flat was still protruding through the sitting room window
of Flat 4A, but the nearby mahogany corner unit no longer played host
to the television that had provided many hours' entertainment—along
with a suitable dance floor—throughout First Year. Dowd's abandon-
ment of the wrecked set some months earlier meant there wasn't much
hope of the lads renting a new one from the same shop as before; at
least not without enduring a severe interrogation. And, as luck would
have it, only one conveniently-located shop rented televisions.

Unfazed by the repercussions from past sins, Goosey found a solution by making a large withdrawal from his bank account and, following a visit to a department store, returned to Flat 4A with a brand new
teletext television. A week later he returned home from college with
a new PlayStation under his arm, by which time his spending spree
was truly beginning to pick up speed. A new wardrobe of clothes followed, and regular visits to Chinese restaurants helped to further im-
prove Goosey's quality of living. But just when it seemed that he had
forgotten he was still living in the wasteland that was Flat 4A, the rug
was firmly pulled out from under him.

One evening, while attempting to withdraw money to fund the purchase of a family-sized pack of Ferrero Roche, Goosey was taken
aback when his card launched itself at him and a message on the
screen told him to, 'Fuck off and come back when you have some
money.' The exact message may have varied slightly, but 'fuck this'
and 'fuck that' were the only coherent words coming from Goosey's
mouth when he barged into the flat and recounted his tale of woe to
the Rams.

And so it came to be that by the last week of October 1997, Goosey
was faced with the prospect of another seven months of sheer hardship and poverty. He had squandered two thousand pounds in six
weeks, was penniless as a result of his actions, and was still—thanks
to the Rams—living in Flat 4A. Could things get any worse? Damn
right they could.

Chapter 21

HARD TIMES AT FLAT 4A

WHEN RAMS and Goosey returned to Waterford for their second and final year of college, they initially attempted to fool themselves into thinking that a fresh lick of paint, coupled with a new kettle and mop, had done wonders for Flat 4A. But with the honeymoon period over and the changing of the seasons fast approaching, a cold and miserable winter would surely give the lads a rude awakening.

Rams recalled the previous winter and, in particular, a bitterly cold evening when he had joined Dowd and a few of his friends for a drink in town. Since Rams only had enough money with him for a single pint of beer, he didn't stay in the pub for long and, making an excuse to leave, he finished up by saying, 'I'm off home now to put my coat on and go to bed.' Although spoken in jest, Rams's statement hinted at the harsh reality of the heating problem in Flat 4A.

Central heaters were located in most rooms, but the amount of heat emitted by these devices was laughable. Rams had figured out in First Year that the best way of heating the sitting room was by switching the oven in the kitchen to its maximum setting and leaving its door fully open so that, within minutes, the adjacent room would be reasonably warm. Unfortunately, the heat from the oven didn't spread to the rest of the flat so the lads were forced to spend almost all of their free time in the sitting room.

By the time Second Year rolled round, Goosey believed he had found a more conventional and satisfactory solution to the lads' heating woes. Following a weekend spent in Cavan, he returned to Waterford and, upon stepping into the flat, produced a small electrical heater from the bottom of his sports bag. It was one of those heaters renowned for eating electricity and, since the lads only had to pay a set amount of three pounds each per week for electricity, they took considerable delight in turning the heater up to its highest setting and leaving it switched on for several hours each day.

One evening a loud knock on the door awoke the lads from their heat-induced slumber. Realising who it was, Winston quickly plugged out the heater, and the Rams kicked it under the couch.

Mickey Rooney walked into the room; a waft of hot air nearly taking his perfectly rounded head off. He had already collected the rent from the other tenants in the building, and Flat 4A was to be his last stop for the evening. The Rams noticed that Mickey hadn't removed his hat and gloves due to the severity of the November weather, which could be felt in all of the other poorly-heated flats.

But somehow Flat 4A resembled a sauna. The Rams was visibly sweating, Winston was fanning himself with a large notepad, and Goosey was sprawled on the couch wearing only a t-shirt and shorts.

Mickey looked shell-shocked.

'Jesus, lads. It's fierce warm in here,' he proclaimed.

'It is indeed,' began the Rams. 'I'm just after making a heap of oven chips and the old oven is just cooling down in the kitchen over there.'

'Oh right,' replied Mickey, wiping the sweat from his forehead and proceeding with the rent collection. A puzzled look was still evident on his face a few moments later when he bade the lads farewell.

Although Rams's smart thinking had saved the day, just a few days later the over-worked heater broke down and the lads were once again forced to watch television with their coats on.

The Antarctic-like conditions in Flat 4A didn't deter Rams's mate, Scott Warner, from staying with the lads. As per the previous college year, Scott stayed in digs during the week and would arrive at Flat 4A every Friday evening, where he would stay two nights before returning to his place on Sunday.

While Rams hadn't two spare shillings to rub together, Scott was even worse off, and this was quite evident from his wardrobe. He could always be seen wearing the same pair of black jeans, the front of which had almost completely faded to white due to excessive wear and tear. Rams's collection of jeans was the envy of nobody, but fortunately he had a good supply of socks. Scott, on the other hand, was the proud owner of a solitary pair of socks. Every Saturday he would walk around Flat 4A in his bare feet while his socks and jocks were spinning in the washing machine upstairs.

'Scott, why do you only have the one pair of socks?' asked the Rams one day, curiosity at last getting the better of him.

'But sure I only have the one pair of feet,' came the reply, and Rams couldn't help but laugh at the logic behind Scott's thinking.

Scott's chilled-out personality meant that he was quite easy to live with. Therefore, Goosey and Winston didn't mind him spending weekends in Flat 4A rent free. He was easy-going and liked most of the same television programmes as the others, which was an important attribute given that the majority of every destitute weekend was spent in front of the television. One programme that Scott loved, much to the bemusement and bewilderment of the Flat 4A trio, was *Buffy the Vampire Slayer*. The lads couldn't understand why Scott liked the show, but they let him watch it all the same.

One day, by way of a joke and wanting to get a reaction, Rams feigned an outburst 20 minutes prior to *Buffy* airing.

'We're not watching that shite today,' he said sternly. 'I've had it up to here with that show the last few weeks.'

Scott's face dropped and Rams felt a wee bit guilty but at the same time couldn't resist seeing how far he could push it.

'I'll tell you what, Scott. If you Hoover the flat, I'll let you watch *Buffy*,' Rams joked.

'No way, Rams,' Scott retorted. Moments later, however, he almost begged Rams to fetch him the Hoover. Rams duly obliged but could scarcely believe that Scott had taken him seriously. Needless to say, Rams's idle threats were repeated every Saturday thereafter, ensuring that the floor in Flat 4A was kept clean and Scott got to see his favourite show.

A few weeks later Rams was forced to fill in for Scott following an altercation with a potted plant. He and the lads had been on the beer for the night and returned to Flat 4A in a fairly inebriated state. Just before going to bed, Rams stuck his head out of his bedroom window, noticed a large plant growing in a pot on the sill, and thought it would be a fantastic idea to uproot it and kick it round the room. Unfortunately, any time Rams thought about doing something stupid, he usually followed through.

The next morning Rams awoke to find that half the contents of the Gobi desert appeared to be scattered throughout his bedroom. A camel seemed to be the only thing missing from the picture. Winston, who shared the room with the Rams, saw the funny side of the delinquent's behaviour, but Rams was astounded by the enormity of the mess he had made. There was only one thing for it: he would have to Hoover the room. Such an act was normally against Rams's religion, but this was an emergency, and so he was forced to swallow his pride and track down the Hoover.

As was the case with the washing machine and dryer, a solitary Hoover was expected to serve the needs of all the tenants in the building. So as to ensure that it didn't magically disappear, Mickey had entrusted the Hoover with a middle-aged man who lived in the flat two doors up from X-File Man.

Hoover Man, as he came to be known, was a grumpy old bastard at the best of times. On several occasions he had come banging on the door of Flat 4A to ask the lads to keep the noise down. Rams, the source of the majority of the noise, seldom heeded his neighbour's requests but would be forced to exchange pleasantries with him every Saturday when borrowing the Hoover on Scott's behalf.

Now on Hoovering duty himself, Rams spent almost an hour cleaning the bedroom before returning the Hoover to his neighbour. Having served a worthwhile apprenticeship under Dowd the previous year, Rams was sly enough to empty the vast amount of clay from the Hoover before giving it back to his grumpy neighbour. The Hoover didn't require bags so all Rams had to do was empty its contents directly into the bin and everything would be fine—or so he thought.

The following evening Hoover Man made a surprise visit to Flat 4A, and the sour expression on his face spelled imminent trouble.

'How's it going?' enquired the Rams.

'Could be better,' growled Hoover Man. 'I was just wondering if the Hoover was working okay for you yesterday evening?'

'Not a bother with it. Thanks again for that,' brown-nosed the Rams, beginning to realise the reason for the visit.

'It's just that a girl upstairs borrowed it an hour ago and it blew up right in her face. She's in an awful state.'

Rams could hear Goosey and Winston laughing hysterically in the background, and he had to work hard to keep a straight face in front of a very concerned and pissed-off Hoover guardian. The pictures running through his head of a girl picking the pieces of a Hoover out of her face didn't help matters.

'I'm sorry to hear that but, as I said, it was working fine yesterday,' said a sympathetic yet smirking Rams.

'I don't suppose you'd have had any reason to tamper with it?' asked Hoover Man, his suspicions increasing by the second.

'And why would I do something like that? Sure, don't I have as much need for the Hoover as anyone else?' retorted the Rams, a hypocritical look of shock now replacing the smirk.

Hoover Man had no choice other than to take Rams's word and, having had a lucky escape, Rams decided not to bother his cranky neighbour again for the lend of a Hoover. Scott must have been relieved by the turn of events but, on the downside, it didn't take long before dirt began piling up on the sitting room floor of Flat 4A. Within a few weeks, the carpet resembled a poor artistic collage featuring hair, toenails, food crumbs and God knows what else.

As a way of temporarily forgetting the poverty and Calcutta-like living conditions, Goosey attempted to cheer himself up one day by preparing a stir-fry meal that looked as impressive as anything served in a top Chinese restaurant. He was almost salivating when he stepped into the sitting room with his dinner in hand. Resting the plate on an arm of the chair closest to the kitchen, he prepared to settle into the same chair while proclaiming, 'This is the nicest meal I've had since moving to Waterfor...'

Goosey's sentence was cut short by the actions of his awkward right elbow, which clumsily collided with the plate, sending it crashing to the floor topside down as the shocked and helpless gastronome watched in silence. He frantically flipped the plate over, but the majority of the food had already merged with the fungus-like carpet. Knowing only too well that such a meal wouldn't come his way again any time soon, Goosey scraped the entirety of the dinner back onto the plate and, after a quick attempt at picking a few toenail clippings out of the similarly coloured rice, he began tucking into the feed, albeit without any further proclamations of what a great meal it was.

Several weeks later Goosey bravely tried to put the unfortunate dinner mishap behind him. Once again he prepared a delicious Chinese meal, and this time he successfully managed to prevent it from landing on the carpet. Having thoroughly enjoyed his incident-free dinner, he briefly stepped into the kitchen before returning to the sitting room with dessert, which consisted of a large bowl of custard. Sitting down on the armchair, Goosey placed the bowl in his lap, and asked the Rams for the television remote control. Rams did as asked but, rather than passing the device, carelessly threw it to his flatmate. The remote struck the bowl, tipping half of the piping hot custard onto Goosey's knee. Enraged, he bolted from the chair and, with the bowl in hand, threw the remaining dessert at the Rams who somehow managed to duck just in the nick of time. The custard hit the wall, creating a series of large stains, which in the future would serve as a daily reminder to Goosey why he shouldn't engage in any further culinary adventures in Flat 4A. He began thinking that all attempts at fancy cooking and self-pampering were doomed and that, if all went well, he'd escape Waterford in a few months with his sanity intact. But his sanity, along with his flatmates', would soon be tested even further.

Chapter 22

THE STALKER

B Y FEBRUARY 1998 Flat 4A was more than living up to its billing from the previous year as being the biggest shit hole any student had ever lived in. The heating was virtually non-existent, the oven door had to be held shut with a stool, custard stains were smeared across the poorly-painted walls, and the flat was so dirty that not even a rat would move in.

The ever-reliable television was the only thing keeping Rams, Goosey and Winston sane, but Murphy's Law dictated that fate would deal another cruel hand sooner rather than later.

It was a typical Thursday afternoon in Flat 4A, and Rams and Goosey had returned home from college shortly after 3 o'clock to spend the remainder of the day rotting their brains with daytime television. Goosey went into the kitchen to make a sandwich but, moments later, popped his head into the sitting room to tell the Rams that somebody had just walked past the kitchen window. Since Flat 4A was on the first floor of the building, and the window, which was located several feet above the sink, looked out onto the top of a shed at the back of the flat, Rams was slightly curious as to who was walking about on the galvanised shed roof. He wasn't, however, concerned enough to divert his attention from the *Ricki Lake* show, where a middle-aged man was about to reveal to his girlfriend that he had been sleeping with her mother for several months.

'Go Ricki, go Ricki,' chanted the Rams in unison with the television audience.

Suddenly the television started moving towards the sitting room window, which was located over six feet off the floor. Rams jumped from the comfort of the couch to save the beloved centre of his universe. Somebody appeared to be tugging at the cable connection from outside the window, so Rams held onto it tightly while calling Goosey for assistance. But before the backup arrived, the cable went slack and Ricki Lake's presence on the television was replaced by an abundance of dots.

Rams and Goosey ran outside just in time to see a Cablelink van speeding away from the building. Having enjoyed a free cable supply for a year and a half, it seemed that the lads' cunning scheme had finally been rumbled. Climbing onto the flat roof, Goosey quickly spotted that the cable had been cut in half. Fortunately, a cheap connector, purchased from a nearby hardware shop a few minutes later, quickly restored cable and harmony to Flat 4A.

Later that evening X-File Man made a surprise visit to Flat 4A. He belatedly warned the lads about two Cablelink employees who had come sniffing round his place earlier that day. They had asked if he was aware that a television cable appeared to be connected from his flat to the one below. Being the good neighbour that he was, X-File Man denied all knowledge of the cable and sent the two men packing. There was no way he'd squeal on his fellow Gillian Anderson fans.

Exactly one week later, Rams, Goosey and Winston arrived home from college to discover that the Cablelink duo had returned and cut the cable again, this time bringing about three feet of it with them. The lads weren't impressed but, nonetheless, bought a measured piece of cable and attached it to the longer piece to restore the picture to the television. Unfortunately, no amount of MacGyver-type bravado would deter the Cablelink men who returned once again a week later and removed as much of the cable as they could manage. Knowing that they were facing a losing battle, the Flat 4A tenants reluctantly decided to face the final three months of college life without television.

Scott, realising that his link to *Buffy* had been permanently severed, immediately sought and located new weekend accommodation.

For the remaining three, however, it wasn't all doom and gloom because the PlayStation now came to the fore as the premier, albeit only, means of entertainment in Flat 4A.

The Rams was something of a video game junkie, and often played for hours on end without moving out of his chair. His parents had bought him and his younger sister, Helena, a PlayStation for Christmas in 1996. Rams initially wanted a PlayStation so he could play a game called *Resident Evil*, which had been released to rave reviews a few months earlier. It was a horror game unlike anything that had come before and, as the following years would prove, was well ahead of its time.

Following a late breakfast at about 10.30 one morning during the festive season, Rams commenced playing *Resident Evil* and, with the exception of perhaps one hour's respite for eating and toilet breaks, managed to continue playing non-stop until 5.30 the following morning. The effects of such a torturous ordeal weren't fully realised until two days later when Rams lost his eyesight completely for over a minute after getting out of bed in the morning. Naturally, such a medical emergency scared the living daylights out of him, but within two days he was once again playing the PlayStation, albeit not in 18-hour stints.

Over a year later Rams was playing *Resident Evil* late one night in Flat 4A. Even though he had completed the game a countless number of times, the addictive and layered nature of the classic lent it an unprecedented replayability level, which meant that Rams never tired of wandering through the same old mansion, shooting the same old zombies.

Winston arrived home from a nearby nightclub shortly after midnight. He had been drinking with a local chap who he had just met and, just to be sociable, had invited the stranger up to the flat afterwards to drink a few more beers.

The Rams's first impression of Ryan was that he had an overly smiling demeanour and seemed a little odd, but he appeared to be harmless all the same. Ryan took an immediate interest in *Resident Evil* and that served to temporarily dispel any niggling doubts that Rams had about his personality. Following several minutes of PlayStation-related conversation, Rams bade Ryan farewell and retired to his room for the night.

The next evening Ryan unexpectedly showed up at Flat 4A. This time his purpose was not to visit Winston but instead to see his new best PlayStation buddy, Rams. The Rams, for his part, wasn't impressed. He didn't like surprises and he particularly didn't appreciate strangers showing up at his door to spend the entire evening playing video games and talking horse shite. The playing games bit Rams could handle, but Ryan's constant chattering and annoying voice could easily evoke violence from those forced to listen to him. At least, Rams presumed, this was a one-off visit. Ryan just wanted to find out more about the PlayStation and, once he'd garnered the necessary information, would, 'fuck off to whatever mental asylum he had escaped from'.

Unfortunately, as the weeks progressed Ryan's visits became as frequent and reliable as the break of day, and there was no getting rid of him. Goosey and Winston would occasionally go to their rooms when Ryan visited, leaving the Rams alone to suffer what was becoming increasingly uncomfortable and infuriating company. By now, Ryan had bought a PlayStation and would spend hours telling Rams about various games he had completed and how he was the best games player in the world, and Rams would nod in agreement while directing his eyes towards heaven and praying for mercy. When Ryan took a break from the incessant talking, he would just sit quietly and stare at whoever was in the room. He certainly went from one extreme to the next, and Rams wasn't sure which of his behavioural oddities was the most despicable.

One night Goosey and Winston once again left Rams on his own with his stalker. It was almost 10 o'clock and Rams thought if he could find a way of getting rid of Ryan then he could enjoy an hour or two of peace before going to bed. He began yawning loudly before standing up and walking towards the hall.

'Jaysis, I'm fierce tired,' he proclaimed, hoping that Ryan would take the hint and go home. But Ryan didn't bat an eyelid and instead continued frantically bashing buttons on the PlayStation control pad.

'I think I'll head to bed,' said the Rams loudly, and he stood in the doorway waiting to see if Ryan would switch off the console and make tracks. Briefly turning his gaze away from the television screen, Ryan said, 'All right so. Goodnight Rams. I'll see ya tomorrow.'

Rams was disgusted that his plan had backfired, forcing him to go to bed early. Meanwhile Ryan continued shooting monsters until the early hours of the morning. Rams half-expected to awaken during the night and discover Ryan standing at the end of his bed, staring at him as if he was the second coming of Christ. And so he breathed a sigh of relief when he heard the door of the flat closing shut shortly before dawn. But Rams made up his mind there and then that something had to be done to permanently dispose of this Michael Myers-type character.

Short of buying a shotgun and letting rip, getting rid of Ryan wasn't going to be an easy task for the Rams. After all, this was the same guy who didn't find it strange that all three young and healthy residents of Flat 4A went to bed every night before 10 o'clock whenever he visited. If that subtle hint wasn't enough to make him leave, what would be?

Two weeks later and the lads were winding down after a stressful day at college, where they had just about finished a project in time for a strict deadline. Suddenly the intercom phone began ringing.

'Ignore it, lads,' ordered the Rams. 'I'm in no humour for that gobshite this evening.'

The buzzing continued for about five minutes before the unwanted visitor finally gave up, and the phone fell silent.

'About time,' said Winston. 'I thought he'd never go. I can go down to the shops to get fags now.'

Winston walked out the flat door, jogged down the stairs and opened the main entrance door, only to be greeted by a beaming Ryan who was just about to press the Flat 4A intercom button for the umpteenth time.

'I've been ringing for ages, Winston,' moaned Ryan.

'Ah, we mustn't have been able to hear ya because of the loudness of the PlayStation,' replied Winston. 'Go on upstairs and say hello to the Rams.'

Ryan's suspicions must surely have been raised further upon entering the flat and observing that the PlayStation wasn't in use, Rams was reading a magazine and Goosey was sorting out his college notes. One could have heard a pin drop in the premises but, despite Winston's blatant lie, Ryan switched on the PlayStation and commenced another six-hour gaming session.

From that night onwards, the lads continued ignoring the intercom when they were reasonably sure it was Ryan who was doing the buzzing. Sometimes Ryan would wait outside the entrance of the building until a resident approached and opened the door, at which time he would sneak in and shoot up the stairs to Flat 4A. He would knock on the door continuously for five or ten minutes, to no reply. But unfortunately Ryan had more patience that an army laying siege to an ancient Greek city. Therefore, he would sit quietly outside the flat door, forcing Rams, Goosey and Winston to be as quiet as mice lest they be heard. Ryan would eventually leave, but the next time the Trojan horse managed to infiltrate the flat, the lads would be in for a telling off.

'I could hear you in here whispering when I was knocking on the door the other day,' he'd say.

Rams would attempt to fob Ryan off with one of his many half-baked excuses.

'Ah, ya must have been imagining things, Ryan,' he'd say. 'Sure all three of us were working late at college.'

Ryan would mumble something under his breath before taking his place in front of the PlayStation, signalling the start of yet another mind-numbing evening in Flat 4A. All good things, however, come to those who wait, and the lads' persistent attempts at keeping Ryan away eventually paid off.

Three weeks had miraculously passed without Ryan managing to breach the security of Flat 4A. Every evening he showed up and every evening the lads were forced to sit quietly in the flat until they were positive that he was gone from the door. One evening the knocking persisted for over 20 minutes without reprieve. Rather than opening the door and beating the living daylights out of Ryan, the lads tip-toed along the corridor to the twin bedroom at the other side of the flat, where they could chat and play cards without being heard by their psychotic visitor.

The knocking finally stopped a while later, by which time Winston was on the verge of winning a game of *Rob the Farmer*. The lads decided to finish the game before returning to the slightly plusher surroundings of the sitting room. Just as Winston gloated in his victory, something clattered the bedroom window.

'What the hell was that?' asked a startled Rams. A second bang resonated from the glass pane and then a third. Winston edged his face towards the window and spotted Ryan on the street below, aiming at the window with a small supply of pebbles in his left hand. He had obviously spotted the light on in the room as he passed by on his way home, and was now intent on making his presence known.

'Rams, your boyfriend wants to see you,' Winston jeered.

'Fuck off, Winston. If it wasn't for you, we would never have met that weirdo.'

After that evening, Ryan never again showed his face at Flat 4A. Unfortunately, Winston didn't learn his lesson and, within a few weeks, another of his acquaintances would leave a more shocking impression on the residents of Flat 4A than Ryan could ever hope to.

Chapter 23

NOT A TYPICAL WEEKEND

SEAN GEORGE Mara II had been promising to visit the Rams in Waterford for over a year, so it was a pleasant surprise when he finally arrived in the city with Terry Kiernan one Friday evening in March 1998. Sight seeing was definitely not going to be on the agenda for the weekend and, following a good night's drinking on the Friday, the lads were in partying form and thirsty again by Saturday afternoon.

As ever, financial constraints confined the drinking to the flat for the first few hours. Goosey was drinking his magical red wine, Rams and Terry were indulging in Waterford's cheapest lager, and Mara was devouring anything that had liquid in it. After a while, Winston and a few of his friends showed up with more drink and a large funnel, which was a common attraction at student parties and was used primarily to drink vast quantities of beer in record-breaking times.

Winston took the first turn with the funnel, drinking an entire can of beer through it in mere seconds. Mara and one or two of the others followed suit, and within an hour a largely inebriated group departed Flat 4A for the nearest nightclub.

Three o'clock in the morning arrived, heralding the return to the flat of Rams, Goosey, Mara and Terry. Rams was as drunk as a fool and immediately made his way to bed. Within seconds, he was in a coma-like slumber. Five minutes later Sean George grabbed a sleeping bag and walked towards Goosey's room, where he picked a spot on the floor and began making himself comfortable.

Meanwhile Goosey and Terry decided to continue drinking for a little bit longer and were just after cracking open some beers when Winston and his mate, Anthony, arrived into the flat to add further numbers to the small party. Anthony had visited Winston at the flat on numerous occasions, and seemed to be a sound and sensible chap. The demon drink, however, can do strange things to normal individuals, and Anthony was already the worse for wear when he arrived at the flat that night. He was about to reach a new low.

Just as the little hand struck four on the clock Winston once again produced the funnel, or 'Yard of Ale' as it was affectionately known. Anthony was first to give it a go and, mere seconds after downing a can of beer, slumped onto the couch with his eyes firmly closed. Nevertheless, he awoke moments later, rose to his feet and walked into the kitchen, closing the door behind him. Goosey and Terry looked blankly at each other, but nothing could have prepared them for what happened next.

Over the course of the next five minutes, several banging noises could be heard from behind the kitchen door, but none of the lads were concerned or sober enough to investigate what the toper was doing. Suddenly the door swung open and Anthony stepped into the sitting room, wearing nothing but his boxer shorts and a disturbing smile. A huge wet stain was blatantly obvious on his boxers and, before a quickly sobering Goosey had a chance to find out where in the kitchen the visitor had taken a leak, Anthony seemed to partially snap out of his hypnotic stance. Looking down at his almost naked body, he began questioning the absence of his attire and seemed to be expecting answers from the open-mouthed and shocked trio of Goosey, Winston and Terry.

'What happened to my trousers? What have ya done with my shoes?' he bellowed.

'Ya took them off yourself, ya fuckin' eejit,' Goosey replied gruffly, his patience obviously waning.

Taking another glance downwards at himself, Anthony seemed to be having difficulty understanding that he was a victim of his own abuse, and he continued with his line of questioning.

'Who fucking pissed on me?'

The lads were still rolling on the ground laughing at this unintentionally hilarious outburst when Anthony stormed out of the room and down the corridor towards the bedrooms.

'I'm going down to ride this fat bitch,' was the final incredulous comment he uttered, and with that he was gone.

Now Rams and Mara weren't exactly what one might categorise as 'fat bitches'. Rams was 140 pounds at best and Mara was perhaps 200 pounds, which perhaps made him the more likely of the two to whom the obviously deranged Anthony was referring.

Mara was on the verge of falling asleep when Anthony burst into Goosey's room and stumbled towards him. Fortunately for Mara, the need for a ride had lasted but a fleeting moment, and now Anthony's main desire was to get a good night's sleep. Stepping across a bemused Mara, Anthony—still wearing his piss-stained boxers—fell onto Goosey's bed with a loud thud. Goosey, upon hearing the commotion, meandered through the corridor and into the bedroom, where he told Anthony in no uncertain terms to, 'Get the fuck out of that bed.' Anthony sobered up pretty quickly, located his missing clothes in the kitchen and, after dressing himself and re-establishing some semblance of respectability, departed Flat 4A and was never heard of again.

The following morning Rams was the first man to awaken in Flat 4A. He had slept like a baby throughout the weird events of the previous night, but he was about to experience a fresh set of confusing and stressful goings on, thanks to the mischievous antics of Sean George Mara II.

Upon rolling over onto his back, the Rams felt the hard, unforgiving surface of his bed dig into his skin. Jumping from the bed in a semi-awake panic, his suspicions were confirmed. His mattress was missing, and there could be but one culprit.

'Mara,' Rams began roaring before even leaving the room. Mara had a habit of playing tricks on the Rams at every given opportunity, so of course Rams was correct in assuming that this prank was his mate's doing.

Rams kicked open Goosey's bedroom door. The loud shouting had awoken Mara, and he sat upright to face the music, a familiar mattress visible under his stocky frame.

'You're some bollocks, Mara. When the fuck did you take that mattress?'

'Sure a man wasn't sleeping too well on that floor, and you were snoring like a dirty mess, so I knew you wouldn't miss it,' said Mara unrepentantly.

Rams marched into the room, reefed the mattress from under Mara, and began dragging it towards the door. Try as he may, however, he couldn't manage to squeeze it through the narrow doorway.

'How the hell did ya get this in here, Mara?' he asked in desperation.

Mara could barely speak due to the tears that were rolling down his cheeks.

'Try turning it on its side, ya eejit ya,' he laughed.

Sure enough, in Rams's half-drunken and erratic state, he had been trying to pull the mattress width-ways through the tiny doorway, and now the realisation of his stupefying error only served to further enrage him.

Two hours later a calmer and more relaxed Rams got out of bed for the second time that day. He went to the nearby grocers to pick up the Sunday paper and a sliced pan. Upon returning, he was in the midst of cooking his breakfast when the rest of the lads began traipsing into the sitting room at five-minute intervals.

As Rams sat down to his delicacy of beans and toast, he grabbed the newspaper and began flicking through its pages.

'The same fuckin' news as last week,' he declared after quickly combing through the entirety of the paper. 'I don't know why I bother my arse buying it.'

It seemed that Mara was in rare form. During Rams's brief sojourn from the sitting room, his so-called friend had plucked the previous week's newspaper from the rubbish bin and placed the majority of its pages between the front and back cover of the newspaper, which the Rams had just purchased. Mara then discreetly began reading the current paper in a quiet corner of the sitting room. Moments later an unsuspecting Rams returned from the kitchen and skimmed through his 'new' paper before scurrilously lamenting the decline of the Irish newspaper industry.

Mara and Terry departed Waterford shortly after noon, at which time the Rams went into the bathroom to wash up. In the preceding eight hours, he had suffered the loss of his mattress and beloved newspaper and then, to make matters worse, he was forced to bin a full packet of ham from the fridge after Goosey explained that Anthony had kindly pissed into the appliance the previous night. Since ham is wet to begin with, it's possible that Rams's beloved slices may have escaped Anthony's reckless hosing. But Rams wasn't prepared to take that chance, so he reluctantly threw the packet into the bin. Unfortunately, the worst was still to come and he was about to discover the loss of something more personal to him than those trivial objects.

Still not fully awake following the two-night drinkathon, Rams was slowly washing his cobwebbed face at the sink when he noticed there was something odd about his reflection in the mirror. At least, it was odder than usual. Staring intently, Rams suddenly gasped in horror. More than half of his left eyebrow was missing. It had obviously been shaved off during the night, and the culprit was the very same person who had been a guest in Flat 4A.

'Mara,' Rams roared, but Sean George was already on a bus several miles from Waterford. At every given opportunity over the weekend, he had successfully made a fool out of the Rams. Not only that but he had narrowly escaped the drunken advances of an apparent mad man who wanted to, 'ride this fat bitch'. Meanwhile Terry had been witness to the same individual stripping down to his boxers and pissing on himself. Not a typical weekend by any means for any of the lads, and certainly one that all of them would remember for some time.

Chapter 24

EXAM TIME

THE END-OF-YEAR college exams were fast approaching, and Rams was anything but prepared. These exams would decide whether he would graduate or not and, having scored none too impressively in some continuous assessment exams and projects during the year, Rams not only had to pass the final exams, but he had to pass them with flying colours or he could wave goodbye to his certificate.

Christmas had spelled the beginning of the troubles. Rams particularly detested Software Engineering. He found the subject matter to be extremely boring, and he wasn't too fond of the lecturer either, which didn't help matters. The Christmas exam accounted for 10 percent of the total grade for the year in that subject and, since Software Engineering was Rams's least favourite subject, it was imperative that he secure a high grade in this mini-exam, thereby easing the pressure a little when the time for the end-of-year exam would arrive.

The only alarm clock in Flat 4A was located at the foot of Rams's bed. Every morning he would spring out from under his duvet, turn off the alarm, take a shower and then wake his flatmates, just before making his way to the kitchen for breakfast. On the morning of the Software Engineering exam, Rams switched off the alarm as usual. Then, contemplating the impossibly boring exam that was but an hour away, he woke his flatmates before crawling back into bed. Surely he deserved a lie-in. Goosey, who wasn't a big fan of

Software Engineering either, decided that if the Rams was prepared to skip the exam and face the consequences afterwards, he would do likewise. And with that, he closed his eyes and attempted to return to dream land, a place bereft of boring exams with taxing questions.

Following a late breakfast, Rams informed Goosey of his plan to make amends for the marks they had so flippantly thrown away.

'We'll just go into college tomorrow and explain that the alarm didn't go off.'

'And what will Dunphy say to that?' asked Goosey, referring to the Software Engineering lecturer.

'He'll have to give us a make-up exam,' said Rams confidently before continuing. 'And it will take him a day or two to prepare a fresh set of questions, by which time we'll have done enough study to get a good mark.'

Rams's plan seemed flawless, and therefore it was with an air of cockiness that he and Goosey approached Dunphy the next day. Rams did all the talking.

'Eh, we missed the exam yesterday and were just wondering if we could possibly make up for it by sitting another one?'

'And how did you miss the exam, lads?' enquired Dunphy while looking none too impressed.

'Well, we only have the one alarm clock in the flat, which normally wakes me up, and then I do give Keith a shout,' explained the Rams. 'But it didn't go off yesterday morning and, since I didn't stir, nobody called Keith and he slept in too.'

The cocky grin now moved from Rams's face to Dunphy's. He couldn't have been privy to the fact that Winston, who had attended the exam, lived with the two absentees and could have woken them. But Dunphy was quite capable of realising when he was been blatantly lied to.

'Well that's too bad, lads. And while I'd love to give you another exam, I'm afraid that's just not feasible.'

'Is there no way we could sit another exam? Even in a few weeks?' asked the Rams in desperation.

'I'm afraid not,' said Dunphy, still grinning and seemingly 'looking for a kicking'.

And that was that. The two Munterconnaught misfits were now down 10 percent in one of the tougher subjects on the syllabus, and it would take a serious effort in the summer exams for them to make up for such a needless cock-up.

Fortunately, the lads were faring slightly better in the continuous assessment for Audio-Visual Studies, which was perhaps the most important subject on the syllabus. Seldom had a week passed without the lecturer, Colin Manning, handing out a new project to his students. Apart from these mini-projects, a significant amount of marks for the year were to be earned from a large group-based project, for which the students were allowed several months to complete. The groups comprised four people and each team member was expected to complete one quarter of the total project. The reality, however, was that this simply was not the case.

The project scope was quite broad, but essentially each group was expected to develop a multimedia product—such as training tutorials—using a range of multimedia software. Most groups consisted of a leader who came up with the project idea. Typically, the leader proved to be a hard worker who was passionate about the project while being the main driving force in bringing it to fruition. Each leader had a right-hand man who also put a substantial amount of work into the project. The other half of the group tended to consist of lazy students who were happy to sit back and let the others get on with it, or well-meaning folk who wanted to help out but weren't assigned any tasks by the zealous leader.

Not surprisingly, Manning would potentially have difficulty in establishing if each student was contributing sufficiently to their respective projects. Each of them was to receive separate marks for the work, but finding a fair way of allocating these marks wouldn't be easy. Nonetheless, Manning reckoned he had a solution. All students were expected to keep a project diary, which would detail their contributions to the project during its six-month duration. Needless to say, just two days prior to the deadline, not one student on the course had made a single diary entry.

But Rams, the cute Cavan hoor, was on the case. That evening he arranged for the other members of his project group to drop up to Flat 4A, where they could write up their diaries together, thereby ensuring that each of them would receive adequate credit for the work done, regardless of their involvement. Of course Rams's idea was of most benefit to himself since he hadn't exactly been the hardest worker on the project thus far. Fortunately, Scott and other good friends were part of Rams's group, so he quietly breathed a sign of relief in the knowledge that their diary write-ups would now correlate with his and thus hopefully camouflage his lack of work on the project.

Eventually all of the write-ups were complete, but unfortunately the diaries still looked like they had been purchased straight out of a shop.

'Manning will never believe we've been writing in these notebooks for the past six months,' Scott lamented.

'Wanna bet?' said the Rams, rising from the chair and walking in the direction of the kitchen. He returned moments later carrying as many condiments as he could manage. Grinning from ear to ear, he commenced an unusual DIY job by opening a bottle of vinegar and sprinkling a generous serving onto the pages of his project diary.

'What are ya at, Rams?' asked Scott in bewilderment.

'A man needs to make this diary look the part,' replied the Rams while squirting a dollop of ketchup between two diary pages. Salt, butter, tea, toast crumbs and all manner of culinary oddities were then smeared, poured and liberally applied to the diary until its pages re-sembled that of an early Christian manuscript that had seen better days and whose author had obviously been a messy eater. Then, as if to add further authenticity to the age of his diary, Rams threw it to the ground, stamped on it until it was covered in dirt and footprints, and then rolled it into a tiny ball before calmly unfolding and flattening it so that it almost resembled a notebook again.

'Manning's going to fail you straight away when he sees the state of that,' said Scott.

'We'll see,' replied Rams confidently.

The day before the projects were due to be marked, Manning turned

up in class with a large bundle of diaries in his arms. He had hoped
that the diaries would aid him significantly in dishing out fair marks.
His facial expression, however, indicated that this had not been the
case.

'All I asked, like, was that you guys keep a diary for the duration
of this project, like,' rang out the strong Cork accent. 'Jesus, these
diaries look like they came straight from the shop into my hands, like.
How do you ever expect to get jobs with this sort of attitude? It's all
right for me, like. I have a job.'

Silence gripped the room as Manning continued.

'As far as I can see, only one of you bothered keeping a diary from
the start of this project, like.'

And there it was. Held aloft by Manning, Rams's diary—in all its
stained glory—was being championed to the class for its authenticity and the diligent work conducted by its writer. As a result, Rams
received an adequate final grade for the project, but that didn't afford
him the time to rest on his laurels. The end-of-year exams were but a
week away, and he had a hell of a lot to do.

Winston was in the fortunate position of being well prepared for
the exams. It also helped that he was one of the more intelligent students on the course, so passing the exams would surely be a formal-
ity for him. Meanwhile his flatmates' approach to studying involved
doing little to nothing for most of the college year but studying just
enough at exam time to salvage their grades. This strategy had worked
flawlessly the previous year. When many students, who had studied
like lunatics all year, failed the First Year exams, Rams and Goosey
couldn't help but take extra pleasure from the success of their mini-
malist approach to studying.

Twelve months later and the lads weren't feeling quite as confident.
It was the night before the first exam, and both Rams and Goosey
were finding excuses not to study. To escape the monotony of the flat,
Rams went for a walk to the nearby shop and, upon returning, found
Goosey writing feverishly on a notepad.

'That's a bit gay,' he said in an attempt to interrupt Goosey's freshly
inspired train of thought. Rams possessed a selfish streak whereby if

he wasn't managing to get any study done, he would try to ensure his flatmates were equally unsuccessful. Goosey, for his part, would often gladly return the favour.

'You're right, Rams,' replied Goosey, packing up his notes and throwing them into a corner. 'Call me in the morning when you're getting up.'

'I'll be up at around 4.'

'That's grand. Talk to you then,' said Goosey as he headed towards his bedroom, seemingly unfazed by the planned early start.

As arranged, Rams called Goosey at 4 o'clock the following morning to study for an exam, which was due to take place eight hours later and for which neither man was suitably prepared. Goosey dragged himself out of bed a few minutes later and immediately began studying at the small desk in his room, by which time Rams had taken up residence in the sitting room, spreading his college notes over the couch before beginning the cramming process.

Having uploaded all of their notes into short-term memory, Rams and Goosey turned up in the exam hall, regurgitated onto paper everything they could recall, and then went to the college bar to celebrate. Three pints later and Rams was telling all around him about the pair's patented study plan.

'I'm telling ya, lads. There's no need to do any revision until the morning of the exam. Just get up at four in the morning and study for eight hours straight. Then, during the exam, write down everything you've learned, and you can forget about it immediately afterwards. Sure I've already deleted everything from RAM, if you'll pardon the pun.'

Rams's study tips didn't convince every member of his somewhat uninterested audience. Nevertheless, he and Goosey prepared for the remaining exams in a similar fashion. Each exam was followed by a celebratory drinking session, but only time would tell if the lads would have anything to celebrate.

The final exam signalled the end of an era as Rams, Goosey and Winston bade farewell to their college friends, Flat 4A and the city of Waterford. It was only fitting that on the lads' last night as students in

Waterford, Dowd travelled over from London to celebrate with them and close the final chapter on what had been two financially difficult yet strangely enriching years.

Goosey had decided to pursue a multimedia degree in London and, prior to that, would once again spend the summer working there while living with his brother, Peter. Rams and Winston were accepted onto a course in Dublin, which would commence the following September. Rams knew it would be impossible to keep in contact with everyone from his class, many of whom he wouldn't see again for years. But time stands still for no man. Dublin beckoned, and little did Rams know at the time that the lure of Ireland's capital would keep him there longer than he ever imagined.

Chapter 25

THE TROUBLE WITH FISHING, DUBLIN AND DISCOS

ALTHOUGH RAMS was saddened to be leaving Waterford behind, he was looking forward to moving home to Virginia for three months, safe in the knowledge that he would be able to live expense-free until September. A summer job in a nearby hotel ensured Rams had a few pounds in his pocket to socialise and indulge in expensive video games that had been pretty much unaffordable while in college.

Like most young adults, Rams had gone through a stage in his teens where he was embarrassed to be seen within 100 yards of his parents. But with the madness of puberty and adolescent torture behind him, he began to develop a new-found respect and appreciation for the two people who had, over the years, made many sacrifices to ensure their three children wanted for nothing.

Therefore, it was fortunate that the hot summer weather of 1998 afforded Rams the opportunity to spend more time with his father by going fishing with him, just as other fathers and sons the world over have done for generations. If truth be known, both senior and junior Smiths were perhaps the world's worst fishermen. Rams couldn't recall his father, Jimmy, ever catching anything other than an old boot. Although Jimmy claimed to have had a few rich summers many decades earlier, Rams remained to be convinced. For his part, Rams was an equally shite fisherman. One summer, during his teens, he pulled several small fish out of the nearby river. Closer examination of such rare form, however, revealed that the exceptionally hot weather had, over the course of a few weeks, reduced the river to little more than a glorified puddle. As a result, fish were practically jumping out of the river, so that even a blind man throwing a paperclip on a string into the water would likely have yielded a result.

One evening Rams and Jimmy went fishing along the banks of one of Lough Ramor's small tributaries. The river was quite narrow, and one careless cast-out from either fisherman would doubtlessly result in his line becoming tangled in a mass of bushes across the river.

Rams and Jimmy were using spinners instead of conventional bait. A spinner generally consists of three hooks, with each hook containing a mini-hook along its length. It acts as a lure and is designed to make noise underwater in order to attract nearby fish. Being the professional fishermen that they were, Rams and Jimmy had only two spinners between them on this particular fishing trip. The backup plan of worms and hooks had foolishly been left behind on the kitchen table, much to the disgust of the female members of the Smith household who made the gruesome discovery shortly after the men had departed to source food for the family.

The fishing trip went well for about 20 minutes. Nothing unusual—such as Rams or Jimmy catching a fish—occurred to spoil the mood. Jimmy was being particularly cautious with each cast-out of the fishing line, ensuring the spinner never came close to the opposite side of the bush-laden river bank. In hindsight, however, he should have paid as much attention to his immediate surroundings.

Holding his fishing rod behind his left shoulder, Jimmy prepared to launch the spinner up the river for the umpteenth time. But he stretched his arm too high and, in doing so, snagged his spinner in the overhead branches of the tree behind him. Jimmy tugged the fishing line, but a number of the spinner's sharp hooks had become firmly entrenched in the tree. He knew the line was likely to snap if he applied much pressure to it, and he would then be forced to call a halt to the fishing earlier than planned. Fortunately, Jimmy had a plan. The car was parked but 20 yards away and, as Rams continued fishing, Jimmy sauntered towards the vehicle and returned moments later brandishing a saw. After climbing the bottom section of the tree, he began sawing the troublesome branch. Meanwhile a mortified Rams stared on in silence, hoping that nobody was witnessing this pitiful excuse for fishing.

Moments later a colossal branch crashed into the river. Jimmy quickly grabbed hold of it by its leaves and pulled it towards him, liberating the invaluable spinner. As one might imagine, the tree was the last big catch of the season, but it didn't dampen the pair's desire to someday 'catch something'.

Over the years Rams also went fishing with Stano and Mara, hoping that they might bring him a bit more luck than his father. But they never did. Mara's fishing rod was almost as much of an individual as he was. It was 13 or 14 feet in length and was composed of several long parts but, given Mara's limited expertise as a fisherman, it provided little, if any, advantage over conventional fishing equipment. The rod certainly wasn't intended for small rivers, where Mara insisted on using it and spending a significant amount of time assembling and disassembling it on each fishing trip.

One glorious evening Mara somehow managed to catch a tiny perch, too small to feed a man but apparently large enough to serve as proof to the Rams of what an extraordinary fisherman Mara was. Mara was still bragging about his glorious catch when he and Rams arrived at Rams's house some time later.

'So what do you normally do with your fish after you catch them?' asked Mara, knowing only too well that such a problem wasn't one that Rams had to face on a regular basis.

'Well if I caught something that small, I'd probably just feed it to the cat,' volleyed the Rams.

Two minutes later the two lads were standing at the bottom of Rams's garden, Mara giddily swinging a tiny fish in front of Miley, the Smith's drooling pet cat. After much teasing, Mara dropped the fish on the grass and Miley pounced on it, feverishly licking the rare treat. Suddenly Jimmy arrived on the scene.

'You're not giving that to the cat, are ya?' he asked before prising the fish from Miley's claws, running it under a cold tap and placing it on a frying pan in the kitchen. Moments later Jimmy looked very much like the cat that got the cream as he tucked into a bland two-mouthful fish supper.

Unfortunately, the end of the summer soon arrived, signalling the end—for another year—of amusing and unproductive fishing trips. And, with the stress-free summer behind him, Rams now had to face the daunting prospect of beginning a new college course in a new city. He had miraculously passed all of his final exams from Waterford Institute of Technology and, therefore, would graduate a few weeks later. Ironically, out of all the exam results, Rams had scored highest in Software Engineering. Goosey had also passed the course; further cementing Rams's view that their study methods were infallible.

Rams hoped the new course he was about to begin would help to further prepare him for a career in computer-related technologies. It was a one-year post-leaving certificate course in computer game development but, because Rams was about to receive a certificate from an Institute of Technology, bureaucratic bullshit meant that he was no longer entitled to a grant. Fortunately, he had managed to retain his summer job for weekends, washing dishes in a hotel kitchen in Virginia. Rams hated the job. It was tough, thankless, minimum-wage work, but at least the few pound earned would help him stay afloat in Dublin.

Of course every time Rams thought he was in financial strife, fate would make matters even worse by delivering a sucker punch right to his gut. Therefore, just six weeks into the college year, roster cutbacks at the hotel resulted in Rams losing his weekend job, meaning that he would have much difficulty maintaining the poor standard of existence he had become accustomed to while in Waterford.

The cost of living in Dublin in 1998 was significantly greater than in Waterford. Rented accommodation was undoubtedly the biggest cost difference between the two cities. Rams was now paying 50 pounds per week in rent and, although this was a lot more than he had been paying in Waterford, at least he now had his own bedroom in what was a small but well-kept three bedroom house in the

Eastwall region of Dublin. Due to Rams's track record in house hunting, Winston had assumed responsibility for sourcing the accommodation for the year, and his childhood friend, Thomas Morkan, took the third room in the house. Tom had also been offered a place on the same course as the lads and, although Rams had met him on only two previous occasions, first impressions suggested that Tom's friendly and chilled-out demeanour would make him an ideal housemate.

The Eastwall trio went shopping in Tescos every Monday evening after college. In Goosey's absence, Tom unwittingly became the victim of Rams's infamous shopping pranks. Every week Winston would compete against Rams to see who could put the most useless and undesired object in Tom's basket without him noticing. Rams's shameless disposition meant that he was seldom upstaged. One day he placed a jumbo-sized packet of tampons in Tom's basket. The messer expected Tom to spot them straight away, but unbelievably he threw a pizza on top of the stowaway product and continued shopping. As Tom made his way to the cash register, Rams and Winston waited in the wings to see what would happen. The shop assistant lifted a pint of milk from Tom's basket and scanned it. A packet of tea bags, a loaf of bread and a bottle of deodorant were then scanned in quick succession. Next came the pizza, and then the tampons were lifted from the basket and scanned.

'No,' Tom roared upon seeing his new purchase in full view. 'They're not mine.'

Rams and Winston could be seen laughing hysterically beside the escalator as an obviously embarrassed Tom waited for the shop assistant to remove the purchase from his bill. It seemed that some college traditions from Waterford hadn't lost their gloss when recycled in Dublin.

The lack of a grant meant that Rams couldn't afford to go out for drinks too often, but one session he didn't dare miss was Stano's 21st birthday celebrations, which took place in January 1999.

Stano had decided against having an official birthday party, possibly because he knew that the sight of Blackie eating his shite years earlier could never be topped. Instead, he and a large collection of his friends gathered in a pub in Oldcastle to have 'a few quiet drinks'. Of course none of the lads knew the meaning of a few quiet drinks and, within a few hours, they were on a mini-bus headed for Virginia. Already half-drunk, the lads barged into a small, quiet bar where a middle-aged chap was singing a variety of country and rock ballads. He seemed to think he was Cavan's answer to Dickie Rock as he sauntered around the bar with a microphone in his hand while attempting to serenade any young woman he happened upon. Approaching Stano's birthday congregation, Dickie stepped slowly through the group while apparently searching for another lady willing to throw her knickers at him.

'Can't hold a candle, can't hold a candle to you,' he sang, before starting into another verse and continuing his perverted walk round the bar until he was once again standing smack bang in the middle of the none too impressed birthday crew. Walking directly in front of the Rams, Dickie launched into another bar of the chorus.

'Can't hold a candle, ca...'

Suddenly Rams grabbed the microphone, singing into it at the top of his alarmingly loud voice.

'Can't hold a candle to you,' he sang, finishing off the chorus with much enthusiasm as the lads hollered and laughed in appreciation of the impromptu yet brief performance.

Naturally Dickie looked really pissed off and, snatching the microphone from the Rams, he made his way to the small stage at the other side of the bar where, according to the Rams, 'he ought to have been all along'.

The lads had seen enough of Dickie's stomach-churning gig, and piled out onto the street in search of a mode of transport to the local nightclub. Almost immediately, a mini-bus pulled up onto the kerb. The lads stumbled on board and ordered the driver to take them to the Lakeside Manor, which was situated about two kilometres outside the town. The journey may have been short in length, but the lads wasted no time in acting the maggot.

Rams got the ball rolling by singing his now favourite song in the whole wide world.

'Can't hold a candle, can't hold a candle to you,' he wailed as two of the lads helped out with the backing vocals. Suddenly Mara pulled Boo Boo out of his seat and, following a brief struggle and much cursing, managed to powerbomb him in the bus aisle. Mara then turned his attention towards Derek Gavin who he promptly powerbombed on top of the helpless Boo Boo. As the two injured parties lay in a heap on the floor, begging Sean George not to land on top of them with his patented 'Mara Splash', the bus reached its final destination.

Leaping from the barely-stationary vehicle, the driver ran towards the nightclub's doormen, screaming and shouting as if Freddy Krueger were after him.

'Don't let any of them fellas in,' he warned the bouncers. 'They're all after going mad on the bus, and I only brought them from Virginia.'

Mara, a big grin on his face as usual, popped his head out through an open bus window.

'Aren't you an awful cry-baby?' he said. 'Going off telling tales to the bouncers.' The rest of the lads laughed and jeered at the driver's expense, but their actions didn't help endear them to the stone-faced bouncers. After initially refusing the lads entry to the nightclub, the head bouncer relented, but served them with a stern warning nonetheless.

'We're going to be keeping an eye on you boys in there,' he said firmly. It didn't take long for the lads to realise that the bouncers weren't going to tolerate the kind of messing that, moments earlier, had almost brought a grown man to tears.

Stano checked his jacket into the cloakroom, and then made a bee-line for the dance floor. He wasn't renowned for his fancy footwork but, on this occasion, a chap by the name of Mister Tequila had temporarily transformed the birthday boy into John Travolta on speed. Unfortunately, the transformation proved to be somewhat fugacious and, as Stano began performing the splits, the tequila appeared to sap the energy from Travolta, leaving him lying powerless on the floor.

Rams and Mara quickly pulled Stano to his feet, but the bouncers had already seen his fall from grace and told the lads that they were, 'skating on thin ice'. Moments later, Stano was in a heap on the floor again, and this time two bouncers picked him up and escorted him outside. The rest of the lads followed in case there would be any trouble.

Having ruled out the possibility of travelling home on the bus that had brought them to the Manor, the lads had rang a bus driver from Oldcastle and arranged for him to collect them after the disco closed. But Stano's unexpected eviction from the premises forced the lads to wait patiently outside, shivering in the cold January breeze while counting the minutes until the bus would arrive.

Of course standing quietly outside the club lasted all of 15 seconds. Stano had forgotten to collect his jacket from the cloakroom. Well actually it was more that the bouncers hadn't been considerate enough to stop with him at the cloakroom before turfing him out. Stano approached the head bouncer at the doorway, and asked if he could go back in to fetch his jacket. His request, however, fell on deaf ears. Subsequent reasoning from a relatively-sober Rams also failed to sway the stance of the hard-nosed doorman. But Stano wouldn't be denied, and made a run for the door. Fortunately, three of the lads managed to grab him before he reached his target, where two massive bouncers were awaiting him with clenched fists. Rams calmed Stano down and told him they'd return the following morning to fetch the jacket. He knew Stano meant no harm, but these bouncers looked like they were itching for a fight, so Rams knew it would be in everyone's best interests to attempt to neutralise the situation.

Having accomplished his mission, Rams's attention was redirected towards the sound of a bus approaching from his left. At last the lift home had arrived. But Stano, seeing an opportunity, made a second daring attempt to retrieve his jacket. Blasting through the doorway, he was greeted by a pair of angry bouncers who used their elephant-like arms to push him straight back from whence he came. Then half a dozen bouncers came out of nowhere, cornering Stano and his entire birthday congregation against a pebbledash wall. As the heavy blows began thundering down on the lads, the floodlights of a minibus suddenly lit up the scene. Momentarily blinded and distracted by the lights, the bouncers stepped back a few feet. The bus driver

162   Ronan Smith

began revving the engine, and this added distraction granted the lads just enough time to break free and run for the getaway vehicle, which was already slowly moving away from the crime scene.

Stano may have been one of the first of the lads to reach the true adult-defining landmark age of 21, but that night he and all his friends had proven yet again that they were a long way from reaching adulthood.

Chapter 26

AN ODJOUS NEW JOB

RAMS'S YEAR of college in Dublin seemed to fly by, and before he knew it he was back working in Virginia as a painter in the same hotel where he'd spent several other summers doing various jobs. The difference this time, however, was that he was no longer a student. It was now time to find a 'proper' job and validate the three years of college education he had successfully completed.

The time spent in Dublin had helped Rams to decide what career path he wanted to follow—he was going to be a webmaster. He had designed his own website as a First Year project while in Waterford and, although the site had been painstakingly hard-coded using a basic word editor, he had enjoyed the experience and continued to maintain and add to the site over the following years. He christened the site *Joystick*, a name synonymous with the site's subject matter of video games.

Joystick combined three of Rams's interests into one enjoyable hobby. His love of video games was well-known, but not many people knew of his interest in writing, a pastime only recently resurrected from his childhood because he wanted to produce a website that didn't just feature his curriculum vitae, a list of 10 things he liked, or paragraphs about each of his favourite colours. There was already enough of that needless shite taking up space on the internet. Therefore, Rams began writing reviews of various PlayStation games. Eventually *Joystick* incorporated news, previews and cheats, and it became a sizable reference guide to all things games-related. It was only after several months of chopping and changing various parts of the site that Rams realised he quite enjoyed the technical work involved in assembling a website. There was a big question mark, nonetheless, over whether he could gain employment doing something he perceived as enjoyable?

Once finished college, Rams no longer had access to a computer or the internet. This meant that he wouldn't be able to update his website but, more importantly, he wouldn't be able to browse webmaster vacancies online. The newspapers carried few jobs of interest, but Rams intended to hold out for his dream job. Some people advised him to take the first computer-related position to come his way. Many graduates may have been happy to follow that advice, but Rams had other ideas. He knew he was capable of excelling in the profession he had chosen for himself—all he needed was to be given the chance to prove it. But with no internet access, his dreams showed no signs of becoming reality.

As luck would have it, Rams's parents came to his aid. After some coaxing from their roguish son, they selflessly agreed to purchase a PC on hire purchase. Rams wasted no time in setting up the internet on the new machine, and he began job-hunting in earnest. Unfortunately, he soon discovered that, despite all the propaganda surrounding the Celtic Tiger and the expanding jobs market, companies didn't seem to be interested in hiring newly-graduated students. If Rams had experience of using three programming languages, one could almost guarantee that a prospective employer would require nothing less than four; if he had four, they wanted five.

The summer soon turned to autumn and, in turn, the autumn gave way to the depressing season that is winter. And still no job for the Rams. Not even an interview. He had been painting for seven months in the hotel and was beginning to wonder if he'd ever get the sort of job he was looking for. And then it happened.

Recruitment agencies were one of a number of things featured on Rams's list of, 'Things worse than Satan himself'. So it was with some caution that he answered a call from an agency one Friday afternoon while at work.

Derek Diamond had received Rams's curriculum vitae the previous evening, and he seemed to be impressed by it. Following a short introduction, he asked Rams a few questions about his experience and skill set, and told him about a three-month contract position that was available with a large accountancy firm. The trouble was that the client in question needed somebody to start on Monday morning. Derek sounded slightly under pressure. He obviously didn't want to disappoint his client, but it was now Friday afternoon and there was no chance in Hell of him interviewing the Rams or anyone else before Monday.

'I'll tell you what,' Derek said. 'You sound like you know what you're on about. Can you start on Monday?'

Rams couldn't believe his ears. Seven months without even a sniff of a job and then he was handed one on a plate. Not only that but the hourly contract rates were more than he could have ever hoped for, and his new employer was a massive international firm with branches in countries he had never even heard of. Rams scoped the hotel reception, half-expecting Jeremy Beadle and a camera crew to show up and start laughing at him.

'I can surely,' he said, snapping out of his Walter Mitty-like daze.

'Great. Now I'm taking a chance on you, so don't let me down,' Derek warned, before arranging to get a contract to the Rams the following Monday.

Rams had definitely turned a corner, but things were moving very fast. He had only the weekend to find a place to live in Dublin, and the idea of a daily commute to the city didn't appeal to him. Fortunately, Lady Luck showed no signs of abandoning the Rams just yet, and by Saturday night he had found a place to stay.

Terry Kiernan was in his last year of a degree course in Dublin. He was living in a flat in Mountjoy Square with Goosey's brother, Trevor, and another lad who had temporarily left the city to work on a construction job down the country. This meant there was a free bed in Terry's place for a few weeks, and Rams was relieved when it was offered to him. He would now have time to settle into his new job before beginning the arduous task of searching for more permanent accommodation.

Monday morning arrived, and the Rams was introduced to the man who would eventually become his boss and friend. Colmán McLaughlin hailed from Donegal and, although he had lived in Dublin for the best part of two decades, he was still Donegal through and through. Rams could never understand how some people from rural Ireland could move to the big smoke and, within a fortnight, be speaking in a posh Dublin accent; all signs of their background and upbringing foolishly erased so as to fit in with their peers. Fortunately, such a travesty would never befall the Rams, and 20 years spent living in Dublin hadn't resulted in Colmán forgetting his roots either. Although he and Rams had grown up a generation apart in different parts of Ulster, they had a lot in common, including their tendency to use certain unusual words, which were seldom heard within the capital.

Rams had only been working in his new position for a few hours, but already the prevalent Dublin accents throughout the office suggested that his colleagues weren't likely to understand him if he were to tell them to, 'Stall the digger' or greeted them with, 'Good man, Horse'. The swearing would also have to be cut back, although he was only ever seconds away from a spectacular 'Fuckin' bastardin' bollocks' outbreak if faced with an uncooperative computer or troublesome colleague.

Corporate Rams was just getting used to saying things like, 'Miserable weather we're having', instead of, 'That's a hoor of a day', when he overheard Colmán speaking on the telephone. Colmán and Rams were expected to launch a major website by the following weekend and, therefore, a mountain of work lay ahead of them. Yet some oblivious individual was asking Colmán if he could commence working on another web-related project.

'I'll be honest with ya,' Colmán said. 'I've an odjous amount of work on here at the moment.'

Rams's ears pricked up. He had never heard the word odjous uttered beyond Munterconnaught or Oldcastle, and he certainly hadn't expected to hear it bandied about in a large corporate environment.

Odjous is one of those fantastic words that can mean different things depending on the situation. It derives from the word odious, which is used to describe something that is unequivocally detestable. Odjous is often used in this same context; 'There's an odjous smell of shite in here', or, 'He's an odjous bollocks', being typical examples of the word's usage in Munterconnaught. Somewhere along the line, however, somebody must have perceived odjous to be too euphonious a word to be wasted on objects of hate or derision. And so it came to pass that the word is now usually used to describe things that are fantastic and in no way detestable. It wouldn't be uncommon for those championing the word to come out with statements like, 'That was an odjous match last night', or, 'She has an odjous pair of tits on her.' Only an Irish man could use the one word to mean completely opposite things.

Rams had already formed the opinion that Colmán was a pretty sound fella, and the fact that they spoke the same lingo further cemented that view. Thereafter, the three-month contract gave way to a permanent position for the Rams. He had found a job he really enjoyed; one that he excelled at. But outside the office Rams was still hell-bent on retaining his wild ways. For the first time in his life he had enough money in his pockets to enjoy himself, and he planned on doing just that.

Chapter 27

A PLACE TO CALL 'HOME'

TERRY KIERNAN and Trevor Geraghty had shared accommodation in Dublin for several years before the Rams moved in with them in January 2000. The flat was a typical student dwelling in that it was functional rather than pretty, but it served its purpose nonetheless and Rams was grateful for the lads' generous hospitality.

Despite the fact that Trevor was Goosey's older bother by less than two years, he and the Rams had seldom spoken anything of note to each other in the 17 years that they had known each other. Only now that they were in their early 20s did the pair begin to form the foundations of a friendship.

Trevor was perhaps more like his younger brother than he would have cared to admit. Goosey had a way with words that almost defied explanation. Without warning, he would often issue a statement mid-conversation that was, in equal measures, observational, side-splittingly hilarious, sometimes cruel and always downright disgusting.

One evening during the good old Waterford years, the lads were drinking cheap cans of beer in Flat 4A. As was often the case on such occasions, the conversation soon began going downhill. Jon Bon Jovi was giving out yards about one of the girls in his class. She was always following him around campus and badgering him with course-related questions.

'It mightn't be too bad if she was good looking,' he lamented.

'Ah, she's not that bad,' Scott said, attempting to be somewhat diplomatic.

'Yeah,' chipped in Goosey. 'I'd love to lick the curry off her 'tash.'

True, the girl had a slightly unfortunate facial growth on her upper lip, but all the lads looked stunned by the graphic magnification of the facts, which had been so eloquently delivered by Goosey. The shock, however, soon gave way to major bouts of laughing and light-hearted accusations of Goosey being 'a sick bastard'.

Fast forward to January 2000 and Trevor was proving to be every bit the poet that his brother was; perhaps even more so. He was also prone to bouts of harmless jeering and seemed to particularly relish in slagging the Rams at every given opportunity. But Rams soon realised that, despite the hard exterior, Trevor was as decent a bloke as one could ever hope to meet.

Three days after moving into the flat at Mountjoy Square, the Rams went for a few pints with his new flatmates. Goosey was also present. Having enjoyed a lengthy Christmas break from college, he was due to fly back to London in the morning and had decided to spend his last night in Dublin so that he wouldn't have to be rushing down to the city from Cavan to catch the early flight he had booked for Thursday morning.

The banter in the pub was as varied and deep as usual, and the first testosterone-fuelled topic of the night concerned women. The lads then switched gears and began discussing football before beginning a heated debate on women who played football and whether any of them were worthy of a 'How's your father?'

Somehow the conversation eventually turned to doors and, specifically, the fine art of breaking doors in. Rams, modest as ever, bragged, 'There's not a door on this planet capable of holding back the Rams.' Trevor began laughing. He wasn't yet accustomed to Rams's ways of going on, and the bold statement was about to be followed up by more senseless ramblings. Years of watching wrestling had resulted in Rams sometimes speaking as if he were being interviewed by Mean Gene Okerlund at Wrestlemania. Rarely a day passed without him using one of his favourite wrestling catchphrases. He had modified most of these sayings so that non-wrestling fans, such as Trevor, would think they were hearing something original.

'Well there's no way you'd be able to break our door in,' said Trevor, referring to the four-inch thick oak door, which kept all would-be burglars from breaking into the lads' flat. This rebuke of Rams's claim would not go unanswered, and he immediately began 'hulking up'.

'Whatcha gonna do… whatcha gonna do when the Ramsmobile and the 24-inch pythons run wild on you?' he asked Trevor while flexing his 'pythons' and attempting to look menacing.

'What are ya on about?' asked a bemused Trevor. 'I'll tell you what. I'll give you a fiver if you can break our flat door in.'

'I'll second that,' said Terry, not wanting to turn his back on a sure thing.

Goosey said nothing. He knew better than to bet against the Rams, a man who would cut his own arm off if the money were right and the audience large enough. And besides, the memory of the unhinged bathroom door in Flat 4A was still fresh in Goosey's mind despite the significant passing of time since that occasion.

The lads dropped by the local grocers on the way home. The hot food counter was always a popular destination after a few pints, and Rams didn't like shouldering doors on an empty stomach. The selection of food wasn't exactly overwhelming. Sausage rolls and spicy wedges were pretty much all that were on offer and, since the sausage rolls looked like they had been cooked in a different lifetime, the wedges were the only viable option.

Rams quickly realised that the Pakistani chap, who was serving the food, had pretty poor English. He seemed to be having trouble understanding Trevor's simple order of 'a portion of wedges'. Now it was Rams's turn to be served.

'I'll have a bucket of wedges, please,' he said cheekily.

The shop assistant looked confused and began pointing at the wedges while seeking confirmation from the Rams that this was indeed what he had requested. Subsequent visits would see the Rams ordering more buckets as well as 'handfuls', 'trailers', 'shedloads', 'spoonfuls' and 'saucepans' of wedges. The challenge every week was to come up with a new, interesting and juvenile way of ordering food.

Terry's college friends lived close by and often joined the lads in the queue for wedges after the pub closed. One night all of the lads lined up at the food counter, each of them ready to unleash a unique order. Terry's mate, Ray, hadn't witnessed the ceremony before and was struggling to contain his laughter as he waited in line behind the Rams.

'Can I have a Wellington of wedges, please?' asked the Rams, his deadpan expression adding further fuel to the fire.

Then it was Ray's turn to order. He was supposed to ask for 'a shoe of wedges', but the Wellington quote had apparently caused him to lose the ability to speak. His face was dark purple as his head shook in silenced laughter and tears rolled down his cheeks at an alarming rate.

'A sho, a shoe,' he cried, before an eruption of laughter-fuelled spittle flew from his mouth and hit the poor shop assistant in the face. Ray was now laughing uncontrollably and had to prop himself up on the counter to avoid keeling over. He eventually dragged himself out of the shop and, upon recovering, promised never to go into a shop with the Rams again.

Just a few weeks earlier, following Rams's first trip for wedges, he and the lads headed back to the flat at Mountjoy Square. Trevor opened the front door of the building, and the others followed him the short distance to the door of the flat; the same door that Rams apparently had 'no chance of knocking in'.

'Stand back,' ordered the Rams. With the path cleared, he took a few steps backwards and charged at the door, hitting it full on with a shoulder. The lads watched as the irresistible force met the immovable object. Following a thundering bang, the door remained in position. Rams hadn't managed to knock it in on his first attempt, but he knew he had come close. A loud cracking sound had confirmed as much.

'Let me take another run at it,' he pleaded.

'Fuck away from it,' said Terry, seemingly annoyed that Rams had damaged a door that could not be damaged.

Terry placed his key into the keyhole but, after much twisting and turning, it became obvious that the lock had been irreversibly damaged. Rams was now beaming with pride, Goosey was sniggering and Trevor looked mildly concerned. Eventually Rams convinced the group that a second decisive running shoulder would provide the only conceivable way of them entering the premises that night. Terry stubbornly conceded, allowing Rams to once again run full-charge at the door. This time he took no prisoners, and the immovable object swung open on its hinges, the lock breaking into two pieces.

The next morning Terry rang the landlord and explained to him that there had been a break-in and the lock on the door would need replacing. In the cold light of day, Rams felt a little guilty over his actions and decided against claiming his winnings from the bet. There was no point in totally taking the piss.

Over the following two months Rams set about securing more permanent lodgings. Unfortunately, a severe shortage of rental accommodation meant this was no easy feat. Stano, Derek Gavin and Thomas Morkan had expressed an interest in sharing a place with the Rams. Stano and Gavin were already living in a cramped flat in Dublin and, therefore, were looking for somewhere more spacious. Meanwhile Tom had just secured a permanent job in Dublin and would be moving from Tipperary in early March.

While flat hunting for himself and the others one evening, the Rams happened upon a familiar sight at an apartment complex, which was located beside Dublin's Millennium Bridge. After following a tenant into the building's foyer, Rams was greeted by three other prospective tenants, each of whom had been asked by the landlady of the vacant apartment to wait downstairs while she attended to some matters on the second floor. Rams was really pissed off because he was once again at the end of a queue, and previous experiences suggested that he may not even get to view the property because of this. For two months he had been looking for somewhere to live, but all the decent advertised properties were leased as soon as the morning papers hit the stands. And of course Rams had work to worry about, which meant he couldn't go flat hunting until after 6 o'clock. There was something deeply depressing about going from door to door on a cold and dark January evening, only to be told, 'I'm sorry. I've just given the place to someone.'

Rams was adamant that he was going to live in the city centre, thereby avoiding the need to use Dublin's atrociously slow-moving public transport. This apartment at the Millennium Bridge was ideally located, and he had no intention of losing out just because he was fourth in the queue to view the place.

One guy in his early twenties was pacing the floor rather impatiently.

'Have you been waiting long?' asked the Rams.

'Over 20 minutes,' replied Mister Impatient, sounding none too pleased. 'This is ridiculous. She buzzed me in from upstairs and told me she'd be down in a minute. And still I'm waiting here.'

'Well I wasn't talking to her, so she never told me to wait. Do you want me to go upstairs and see what the hold-up is?' asked Rams, a crafty idea entering his head.

'Yeah, that's a good idea,' said Mister Impatient.

'Right so. I'll be back in a few minutes.'

Rams could barely keep a straight face as he bounded towards the elevator. The three gobshites standing inside the front door had just unwittingly allowed him to skip the queue and attempt to secure the lease while they awaited the appearance of a phantom landlady.

The phantom answered Rams's knock on the apartment door. She seemed annoyed that he hadn't waited downstairs, but he feigned ignorance and she then apologised for keeping him waiting. Mrs. McNamara was in her early fifties, and Rams's initial impression was that she was overly serious despite appearing to be a bit dizzy. She showed Rams around the apartment. It was modern and clean but there were only two bedrooms, which would necessitate the lads sharing. Tom had already agreed to, if necessary, share a room with the Rams, and Stano and Gavin would take the other one. Ideally, each of the lads would have their own room, but affordable four-bedroom city centre apartments were almost a thing of the past in Dublin.

Having almost inadvertently purchased a house in Waterford a few years earlier, Rams carefully interrogated Mrs. McNamara to ensure that she wasn't attempting to trick him into taking out a 30-year mortgage. He then spent several minutes explaining to her that he and his friends were professionals who enjoyed the quiet life and hated parties of any sort. Although seemingly taken in by Rams's bullshit-laden dose of logorrhoea, McNamara suddenly announced that she had, 'sort of promised the place to another chap', earlier that evening. But Rams knew enough about greedy Dublin landlords to realise that money talks, and he quickly produced over 600 pounds from his wallet, handed it to McNamara and told her he'd have the rest of the deposit by the end of the week. Suddenly the other 'chap' was but a memory, and Rams was the new leaseholder in Number 29.

Walking from the elevator and towards the foyer, Rams could see that the other prospective tenants were still waiting patiently for McNamara to show them around the apartment. Rams had spent over 20 minutes upstairs and, therefore, would surely now be at the receiving end of numerous questions. Fortunately, quick thinking was something he had never been slow at.

'Well, what's the story?' asked one of the irate flat-hunters.

'Ya won't believe it,' said Rams, taking a deep breath before unleashing a myriad of lies. 'Yer wan upstairs shows me around the entire apartment and then tells me that someone has already taken the place. She's obviously off her bloody rocker.'

Screams of outrage filled the Rams's ears. All three of the injured parties had been waiting to view the apartment for close to an hour, and now it seemed that the place had been leased all along.

'Look, I'm out of here,' said Rams, feigning anger and adopting a vicious scowl on his face. 'This one has wasted enough of my time.'

Rams threw open the front door and stepped onto the street, leaving three open-mouthed and distraught individuals in his wake. It had been a close shave, but the smart Cavan man's deceitful lies had been convincing enough to prevent him from receiving a lynching.

Finally the Rams had a place to call 'home' in Dublin. Work was going well and he had money in the bank. Now it was time to do something that was long overdue.

Chapter 28

LONDON'S CALLING

IN THE short space of a year, the Rams had transformed from an impoverished student into a successful graduate with a responsible job in a large international company. He was earning a good wage for someone his age and no longer had to scrimp and save to put food on the table, and this newfound prosperity afforded him opportunities to do things that had never been possible in the past.

And so it happened that one Friday evening in August 2000 the Rams stepped onto an aeroplane for the first time in his life. His chosen destination was predictable but exciting nonetheless. He had considered moving to London a year earlier to begin his career but factors, such as money and the uncertainty of quickly securing employment, soon rendered that prospect unviable. Now Rams's reasons for visiting London were purely one-dimensional. A piss-up of the highest order was on the cards.

Goosey and Dowd were waiting in Heathrow Airport when the Rams touched down on the Queen's soil. Dowd was carrying a six-pack of beer, which the trio began tucking into as soon as they stepped onto the tube. Rams's luggage consisted of just enough clothing to keep him going for the duration of his visit, but there would be no time to drop the bag off at the lads' flat in Bayswater. Several tube stops and a couple of beers later, Rams followed his friends from the train to an Australian bar in nearby Acton.

It was very late into the night before the lads returned to Bayswater,

at which time plenty more drink was consumed. Rams woke with a
start the next morning and attempted to piece together the events of
the previous night. The other lads were also soon awake and it didn't
take long for the drinking to kick off again. The large flat soon filled
up with Irish revellers. Flan, Dorgan and Hartley, who also lived there,
were present along with Rams, Goosey and Dowd. Rams wasn't the
only weekend visitor to Bayswater. Two Irish men, John Geary and
Barry McGovern, arrived on the scene and were now supping on cans
as if there had been an alcohol drought in recent times. They planned
on spending the night in London before flying out early the next
morning to begin a round-the-world adventure.

Spirits were high and livers mildly pickled by the time the large
group of lads shipped out to The Swan in Stockwell. The Swan nightclub had long been a favourite haunt of the Irish expats in London.
Seldom had a Saturday night passed without Goosey, Dowd, Flan,
Dorgan and Hartley making an appearance. Over the course of the
night, pints were drank, women were chatted-up and more pints
were drank until eventually all of the lads were very much worse
for wear, and none more so than the Rams. He stood waiting outside the club for Dowd who had told him he'd meet him there. But
patience wasn't a virtue often associated with the Rams. He could
have slept standing up and, at that moment, just wanted a bed for the
night. Flagging down a taxi, he hopped into the back seat and barked
instructions.

'Bring me to a hotel, Merchant.'

Rather than bothering with the formalities of first names, Rams
tended to call most people—strangers and friends—either 'Merchant'
or 'Horse'. 'Horse' was a common naming convention amongst Cavan
men, and 'Merchant' was first used by Stano and thus became popular
over the years amongst his circle of friends.

As it happens, the Rams could have called the taxi driver, 'Ming the
Merciless', and chances are he wouldn't have batted an eyelid. Like
many other taxi drivers in London, Merchant wasn't a fluent English
speaker, but he had enough of a grasp of the language to know what
'hotel' meant.

After a failed attempt at locating the 'Hotel Merchant', the taxi driver dropped Rams off on a street littered with over half a dozen small hotels. The time on Rams's wristwatch was a blurred mess, but he knew that if he were any later looking for a hotel, he'd be in time for breakfast.

Five hotels later and Rams was still meandering along the street, praying that he could avoid homelessness on what was only his second ever night outside of Ireland. Each hotel was either full or completely beyond his budget, and Rams was beginning to feel like Joseph of Nazareth walking the streets of Bethlehem, only without the pregnant wife or holier than thou disposition; either of which might have helped him get a room in this modern London setting.

Rams woke with a start the next morning and looked around his unfamiliar surroundings. He was in a tiny but clean hotel room. Suddenly some flashbacks began jogging his memory. He remembered catching a taxi to a street lined with hotels, being told on several occasions that there was, 'no room in the inn', and—just before drunkenly beginning a search for a stable and a few donkeys to snuggle up to—finding a vacant hotel room for 50 pounds.

Okay, so the Rams now knew how he had arrived at wherever the hell it was that he had arrived. But he had other problems aside from the fact that he hadn't the foggiest notion where he was. He didn't know the lads' address. The details were on his mobile phone, but he'd cleverly left that gimcrack sitting on a table in the place that he was now trying to find. All phone numbers were stored on his mobile, so it looked like he was well and truly up shit creek with no toilet roll.

What if he had to stay in this tiny hotel room for the rest of his life while pictures of him popped up on milk cartons and lampposts all over Ireland? And the television reconstruction of his disappearance would surely embarrass his family by portraying him as a drunk who was last spotted outside a club in London trying to chat up girls while slapping himself in the face to stay awake.

Suddenly Rams slapped himself in the face. *'Enough of this bullshit. Time to formulate a plan.'*

'You're a genius, Rams,' he said aloud seconds later. One of the few numbers Rams could easily recall belonged to Goosey's parents back in Cavan. After trying to work the hotel telephone, Rams gave up on it and hit the streets in search of a phone box. Ten minutes later he found one but was now faced with the daunting challenge of figuring out international dialling codes, which were a banana skin he'd failed to anticipate. After some assistance from the nice Directory Enquiries lady, Rams got through to the Geraghty household, obtained the number he needed and then at last got speaking to Goosey.

Dowd was more familiar with the geographic landscape of London so he took the phone receiver from Goosey and attempted to direct the 'stricken aircraft to safety'. He asked the Rams to describe all he could see from the phone box and, armed with this information, deduced that Rams was located at Pimlico, two tube stops away from where all the lads had been the previous night. Dowd instructed Rams on which bus would bring him most of the way to Bayswater, and with that Rams was on his way.

After disembarking from a bus close to Bayswater, Rams was almost at his final destination. Almost—but not quite. He didn't have a clue which direction he should be walking in. Therefore, he began asking people on the street for directions, but they were either fellow tourists or locals who refused to assist him. Rams knew he was close to Dowd's flat, but wandering aimlessly wasn't producing any results. He popped into a corner shop and was greeted by a Pakistani man. After purchasing some chewing gum, Rams showed the assistant the address he had scrawled down while talking to Dowd.

'I'm sorry. I don't know this place. Maybe if you go to the shop next door my brother will be able to help you.'

Rams laughed to himself on the way out the door.

'Seven million people in this city, the prices of commercial property shooting through the roof, and here are two Pakistani brothers running rival convenience shops on the same street corner in central London,' he thought.

Back at the flat in Bayswater, Goosey and Dowd were a little worried about their guest from home who hadn't been seen in almost 10 hours. Suddenly the Rams marched into the sitting room, a bobby hat on his head, another one in his right hand, and six cans of beer and a packet of rashers in his left.

'Why the sad faces, lads? Come on, it's time to start the drinking.'

Rams's first trip to London had undoubtedly been a barrel of fun, but he only had to wait four weeks before making a triumphant return. He was sitting at his desk at work on a Thursday afternoon when he heard about a sale on Ryanair's website. Flights to Luton Airport in London for that weekend were just one pound before taxes. Suddenly Rams was inspired to revisit the lads. He rang Goosey and then Dowd to confirm they'd be in Bayswater at the weekend and, following two positive replies, his mind was made up and he booked a flight immediately. He would be leaving the following afternoon and would return on Sunday. But with the flights so cheap, perhaps he could persuade a friend to go along with him.

Winston had returned from London four months earlier. He had spent a year working there as a programmer and was now working in a similar role in Dublin. Shortly after returning, he went for a pint with Rams and Tom to catch up on recent goings on. They were only on their second pint in a bar called Turk's Head when the Rams began yawning. He hadn't slept well the previous night and was now a little tired.

'I could really do with a seat,' he said, looking fruitlessly around the surprisingly busy bar. As he continued conversing with his two friends, an empty place suddenly appeared in his peripheral vision. Wasting no time, Rams flung himself onto the vacant stool and continued warbling on to the lads about the state of the nation and the price of beetroot. Within seconds, he realised that his stool was a bit wonky and appeared to be moving under him. Jumping to his feet, he looked down to where he had been sitting. And there staring back up at him was a shocked and speechless young man.

'Jaysis, sorry man. I thought you were a stool,' Rams said in a rather matter-of-fact manner. It was almost as if he regularly sat on strangers' heads in the belief that they were in fact bar stools.

The young man was still too shocked to reply. He had only just knelt down on his honkers to speak to his girlfriend when the Rams appeared from nowhere and planted his 10 stone frame on top of his head. Meanwhile Winston and Tom were almost shitting themselves as they laughed and sniggered at Rams's expense.

'Well what was he doing going round looking like a stool?' snapped the Rams upon returning to his original standing place.

A few months later Rams and Winston landed in Luton Airport courtesy of Ryanair's cheap flights. After a considerable amount of time spent navigating the tube, the pair arrived at Bayswater, full of life and ready for a good night out. Once again the venue of choice was The Swan, and once again the Rams managed to get ridiculously lost at the end of the night. He couldn't manage to stop a taxi and hence was forced to walk the streets of London in the hope of running into a familiar face. After what seemed like an eternity walking, Rams shuffled onto a motorway. As he stood in the middle of the four-lane road, traffic approaching him at speed from two directions, he threw his arms up in the air in despair and roared, 'Where the fuck am I?' The walking continued for over an hour and Rams got to see parts of London that most people didn't even know existed. Shortly after taking a piss in a junkyard of all places, Rams recognised a building, which he was fairly sure was close to Dowd's flat. He continued walking, and a few minutes later saw the one and only Winston Ralph across the road. Both men had by now walked themselves sober, but within 20 minutes they managed to find the flat and escape London's dark streets.

Saturday night promised to offer something a little different. Lisa Hetherton had attended primary school years earlier with the Munterconnaught trio, and was now based in London as a nurse. Some of her friends were throwing a party at Saint Mary's hospital accommodation at Paddington on Saturday night, and she had kindly invited the lads along. They didn't need to be asked a second time. Beer and nurses always formed a genius tag team no matter what way you looked at it.

The lads were well tanked-up by the time they arrived at Paddington. The party was already in full swing and a large number of people were drinking away and enjoying the banter. The boys didn't take long to make themselves at home. Dowd was chatting away to various people in the sitting room while Goosey and Winston were putting in a bit of groundwork with a small group of nurses in one of the bedrooms. Rams was at the other side of the room, high as Icarus with beer and holding court as only he knew how. As he began telling some girls a story that may have been true but for which he hadn't yet decided the ending, a bit of a commotion could be heard outside the room.

Rams stood up and strolled over to the doorway. The sight awaiting him at the opposite end of the corridor was completely unexpected.

Several members of London's Specialist Firearms Command, otherwise known as CO19, were walking around the apartment. These guys are London's equivalent to the SWAT units deployed in the United States. They were tooled up with assault rifles, stun grenades, full body armour, the works, and they definitely looked like they meant business.

The Rams, however, was unfazed and unleashed a loud roar that silenced everyone at the party.

'There's a bomb, there's a bomb!'

There's an unwritten rule that if you're at a party in London, which has just been invaded by a SWAT team for an as yet unclear reason, and you have a strong Ulster accent, then it would be rather advisable not to start shouting the odds about there being a bomb on the premises. The Rams, it seemed, was not privy to this rule and had just unwittingly put his life in danger.

Rams returned to the bedroom immediately after his big announcement and calmly took his original seating place on the bed. You could have heard a pin drop in the apartment and then, as if things weren't bad enough, he sensed an ominous presence to his right. Turning his head in that direction, Rams was slightly taken aback to find three assault rifles pointing at him, their owners ready to take him out if he put another foot wrong.

Waving his right arm about, Rams attempted to diffuse the situation.

'I was only codding,' he bellowed.

Three red dots, however, remained firmly fixated on his torso. Suddenly a middle-aged woman arrived on the scene and began investigating what the hell had just gone down. She appeared to be the landlady or caretaker of the building, and understandably she had a face like a pissed-off tiger on her. After a short conversation in the hallway with the SWAT team, she stormed back into the bedroom.

'Right. You, out,' she screamed at the Rams. 'And you too,' she said, pointing her witch-like finger in Goosey's direction.

The pair didn't need to be told a second time. The adrenaline was pumping as they left the building only to spot a helicopter circling overhead, strong lights illuminating their path.

'You really did it this time, Rams,' laughed Goosey as the noise from the helicopter rotors faded in the background.

Unsurprisingly, Dowd and Winston didn't hang around the party, which had by now degenerated into a funeral-like occasion. Indeed, the Rams had come devilishly close to providing the corpse.

Dowd discovered the reason behind the storming of the castle when he bumped into Lisa a few weeks later. Apparently a large group of off-duty cops had been at the party. One of them heard what turned out to be a starter pistol being fired in the vicinity of the apartment. Rather than properly investigating the situation, the gobshite rang headquarters and implied there was a mad man with a gun on the loose at the party. There may indeed have been a mad man on the loose, but he didn't have a gun—just a loose mouth.

It had been a close shave, but Rams had miraculously escaped punishment for a reckless act of stupidity. But had he at least learned a valuable lesson about when to keep quiet? No is the short answer. In fact, if anything, it was worse he was getting.

Chapter 29

THE SEASON OF GOOD WILL

C HRISTMAS SEEMED to approach in no time. It didn't seem like a year had passed since the millennium celebrations. The lads had commenced those particular festivities in earnest on Christmas Eve, and the night had been such a riot that New Year's Eve could only ever end up as an anti-climax in comparison.

Christmas Eve is usually a good night to go for a drink in Ireland. The pubs close at midnight, but that just provides an excuse for many people to drink much faster than usual and be nicely jarred before retiring early in anticipation of the following day's big dinner.

One of Virginia's numerous pubs had been renovated in the days leading up to the millennium, and half of Munterconnaught decided to visit the establishment on Christmas Eve to see what exactly had been done with the place. The refurbishment turned out to be quite extensive. The floor had been completely retiled, a new marble bar had been put in place, and the entire pub had been impressively remodelled and painted.

The evening started quietly enough and everyone was quite civilised for about an hour until one of the lads arrived back from the toilets with a pick in his hands. The usefulness of a pick cannot be underestimated when deployed for gardening and small construction jobs. But when a pick turns up unannounced in the middle of a crowded pub, trouble is not far behind. The pick was greeted with rapturous applause from the delighted crowd, and it was then passed around the pub like a pet monkey. A large amount of clay was stuck to both ends of the pick's head, but that didn't prevent some lads from dipping it into their mates' pints when they weren't looking.

Just as the popularity of the pick was beginning to wane, Martin Brady returned from the toilets with a box of loose floor tiles in his grasp. Apparently, prior to finishing up for the Christmas break, the builders had abandoned the tiles and the pick in a small room adjacent to the toilets, and of course the door had been left ajar as if to invite the devilment that was but moments away.

Almost immediately, the tiles were distributed amongst some of Munterconnaught's biggest lunatics, many of whom then began re-enacting scenes from their favourite kung-fu movies. One lad would hold either side of a tile and his accomplice would drive his elbow into the tile, breaking it in two. Within a few minutes, the floor was littered with broken tiles, and the manager of the premises was frantically scanning the area, wondering where the tiles had been pulled from and why this shower of bastards were seemingly out to destroy everything he had worked so hard to put together. His investigation soon led him to the Rams and his friends who were standing beside a small mountain of broken tiles.

'Which one of you lads did this?' he demanded.

Dowd made a quick scan of the pub, spotted some strangers just a few feet away, and then deviously shifted the blame.

'I'm not sure who it was, but that crowd over there have been making a lot of noise all night.'

The manager immediately stormed over to the group of unsuspecting lads. Naturally an argument ensued, and the real troublemakers laughed at the spectacle before looking for new ways to entertain themselves. The wait was short-lived.

The pick had once again become the must-have accessory of 1999 and was being passed about from Peter to Paul. Suddenly one of the strangers, fresh from the extensive bollocking he'd received from the manager, found himself holding the weapon. He looked at it for a moment and then, within the blink of an eyelid, lifted it above his head and brought it crashing down through a pint of Guinness and into the newly installed marble bar counter. It was now after midnight and the pub was on the verge of closing for the night. Thus, amid the commotion from punters demanding more drink, this act of vandalism went unnoticed by the manager. Then, as if to create a diversion from the scene of the crime, two of the more civilised individuals amongst the Munterconnaught group began beating the shite out of each other for no apparent reason. The pair fought the length and width of the bar before moving outside to continue trading blows. They were quickly followed by the remainder of the bar's customers who had transformed into blood-hungry spectators and were now shouting and egging on the combatants. This presented the pub's manager with an unexpected opportunity to close the front door and bolt it shut. He had experienced a night like no other; the events of which he hoped would never be repeated.

With Christmas 2000 only around the corner, Rams wondered if anything could match the insanity witnessed the previous year. He finished up work for Christmas at 3 o'clock on Friday, three days prior to Christmas day. A group of his workmates joined him across the road in Dicey Reilly's pub for a few festive drinks, and Goosey arrived an hour later, having just stepped off a flight from London.

By 10 o'clock most of Rams's colleagues had either gone home or were on the verge of forgetting where home was. One of the few remaining die-hards, Glen McArdle, was about to stumble out the door when, as if by magic, Dowd appeared. With the obligatory introductions and resultant 'one for the road' drinks out of the way, Glen once again attempted to head for home. He was shaking hands and hugging everyone on his way, and soon came towards the Rams to bid him farewell. Rams, however, decided to take the initiative and wrapped his arms around Glen's lower back. Glen was a reasonably big man, over six feet tall and considerably heavier than the Rams. But that didn't concern the smaller man who, with his arms still wrapped around Glen's lower back, lifted his colleague off the ground. Picking Glen up was the easy part. Holding him in mid-air, especially after several hours' drinking, would prove impossible.

With a loud bang, the pair crashed through the nearby bar table, a

multitude of drinks spilling everywhere. As the two lads dusted themselves off, a Chinese waitress approached carrying a mop and bucket.
Rams considerately placed one of his beer-drenched feet on a chair in
a half-assed attempt to get out of her way so that the she could easily
mop up the mess.

'Your foot, your foot,' she shrieked.

Rams, in his drunken stupor, thought she was referring to the foot
that was still on the floor, and with that he placed both feet on the
chair and stood upright, much to the annoyance of the waitress.

At 3 o'clock in the morning the lads decided to call it a night,
and they walked the 10-minute journey to Rams's apartment at the
Millennium Bridge. Goosey had travelled light and was only carrying a sports bag with him. Dowd, on the other hand, never did things
by half, and had brought a large portion of London home with him in
two gargantuan rucksacks. Upon arriving in Dublin earlier that night,
he had followed a resident into the apartment block beside the bridge
and, since Rams was in Dicey's and hence there was no way of gain-
ing entry to the apartment, he dumped his bags on the second floor
just outside the lift. He then hopped in a taxi and headed for Dicey's.

'Where did ya say ya left your bags?' asked Rams for the umpteenth time as they entered the apartment block.

'Wait a minute,' said Dowd, a worried expression suddenly cloud-
ing his face. He looked down the corridor and then towards the front
door. 'This isn't the building I was in earlier.'

'Are ya messing?' asked the Rams in the hope that Dowd was playing a practical joke.

But Dowd wasn't messing, and a minute later the lads were walking the streets of Dublin looking for an unlikely needle in a haystack.

'Sure ya were in the flat a few months ago. How did ya end up going to the wrong building this time?' inquired Rams. Dowd didn't
reply. He was now staring at the Ha' Penny Bridge, which was but a
stone's throw from its Millennium Bridge counterpart.

'This is the bridge,' he gleefully declared.

Seconds later Rams and Dowd were standing outside an apartment
block where Dowd was adamant he had left his belongings. With no

way into the building, it was only a matter of time before the Rams suggested he knock the door in with his shoulder. Fortunately, a resident showed up seconds before Rams had a chance to bring his plan to fruition, and the two desperados followed her into the foyer. Quickly locating the elevator, the pair cruised up to the second floor where Dowd's luggage was awaiting them. Rams laughed aloud when he saw the bags. They were about as conspicuous as an elephant walking down Grafton Street. No Shame had obviously just flung the bags into a heap on the floor and abandoned ship. Luckily for him, his belongings were undisturbed.

'That's a relief,' Dowd declared. 'I have over two grand sterling in those bags.'

'*Fuckin' typical*,' thought the Rams, raising his eyes to heaven.

The next morning the lads discussed how to get home to Cavan for Christmas. They were sitting in a hotel bar close to the apartment. Not just any hotel but one of Dublin's most expensive and upmarket establishments. Eight pints later it was decided that getting a taxi to Kells was the only way to travel. Goosey's brother, Trevor, would surely enjoy picking them up there and driving them the rest of the way home.

After agreeing on a pick-up time and a price of 50 pounds with a local taxi man, the lads ordered more pints. Rams was by now threading on thin ice with the bar manager. The more he drank, the louder he became, and he was perhaps already Ireland's loudest man without any drink on board. The loudness might have been excusable, but the profanity wasn't, and certainly not in one of the city's trendiest hotels.

Rams was regurgitating one of his infamous stories, his friends laughing along while the manager glared at him across the bar.

'Well I fuckin' know for a fact that the lying bastard was…'

The manager had heard enough and was compelled to interrupt.

'I'm sorry. I'm going to have to ask you to refrain from cursing,' she said sternly. 'There are other guests here, so any more of that and you'll have to leave.'

'No problem at all,' said Rams, adopting a gentlemanly persona in an attempt to get back on her good side. 'I'm very sorry about that. It won't happen again.'

And it didn't; at least not for another 20 minutes. Rams bit his tongue and managed to successfully converse with his friends without resorting to profanity, making his behaviour somewhat reminiscent of a civilised human being. For the duration of this saint-like performance, however, the bar manager was nowhere to be seen. Meanwhile the Rams was finding it increasingly difficult to maintain this facade. Words like 'fuck' and 'bollocks' were tickling his voice box, begging for release. Finally the manager reappeared at the exact moment that Rams, unable to restrain himself any longer, delivered a sentence packed with more filthy language than a Roddy Doyle novel.

Taking one swift look at the glaring harridan behind the bar, Rams knew it was time to depart the premises. The taxi arrived a few minutes later, and the lads journeyed to Kells where more drinking, eating and loads more shouting ensued. Christmas had arrived and No Pain, No Shame and No Brains planned on enjoying every minute of it.

Chapter 30

THE RATTLIN' BOG

THE BEGINNING of 2001 heralded changes aplenty. Stano didn't return to the apartment in Dublin after Christmas. He had moved back to Munterconnaught so that he would be closer to work, which was now concentrated mainly around the Kells region. And the year wasn't a week old when Dowd flew to Australia, a minimum of 12 months' travelling ahead of him.

Although Dowd would be missed, Rams only ever saw him a few times a year since he finished college, and he knew they'd keep in contact throughout the year via email. Stano's departure, however, would prove more apparent in the short-term. He and Rams were perhaps not quite as close as they had been during their school years, but living together for nine months had afforded them the opportunity to reaffirm their long-standing friendship.

Living with Stano had been great fun. Munterconnaught men were renowned for their sense of humour and ability to make people laugh, but Stano was funnier than most. He had an uncanny ability to make almost everything he said seem funny. Even when he wasn't intentionally attempting humour, Stano usually managed to bring it to the table in spades, and this undoubtedly made him the funniest person Rams had ever known.

Stano moved home several days before Christmas. But in true slapstick fashion, going home turned into a four-day event.

It was a Friday morning, and Rams had just crawled out of bed. He had arranged to take the day off work so he could go out the previous night for a big session, enjoy a lie-in on Friday morning and be well rested for his work Christmas party later that evening. But despite the extended stay in bed, the Rams was suffering. The big session had evolved into an outrageous session, resulting in one.of the worst hangovers of all time. Fortunately, he wasn't the only one suffering. Stano soon joined him in the sitting room, looking as rough as a sheet of sandpaper and smelling like he'd drank Dublin dry the previous night. He was supposed to be working with his father on a building site in Kells but was running slightly behind schedule by several hours. He looked in the fridge, spotted a 12-pack of lager, threw one of the cans to the Rams and opened one for himself. Two hours later the pair of layabouts were two-thirds of the way though the cans.

'What are ya at, Stano?' asked the Rams, noticing him fidgeting with his mobile phone.

'I'm just going to call the auld lad and tell him I won't be in today.'

Rams couldn't hide his laughter. It was 2 o'clock in the afternoon. Stano usually began work six hours earlier.

'I'd say he has a rough idea you won't be in,' Rams chuckled.

But Stano was not to be deterred and he made the vital call, after which the drinking continued. The next few days began in a similar fashion, with Stano full of good intentions to drive home to Munterconnaught, but it just wouldn't happen. Rams was proving to be a bad influence, and he encouraged his friend to remain partying in the capital with him for several nights. Eventually Stano made it home on Tuesday, and his tenure as Rams's flatmate was over.

Despite moving out of the apartment, Stano would return to Dublin for the occasional night on the town, and Rams, for his part, would meet him and the rest of his old school friends in Oldcastle every three weeks or so. Unfortunately, nights out in the lads' former favourite haunt, the Springs, had become rather unfashionable. The growing number of new pubs and clubs in nearby towns had reduced the attractiveness of the nightclub to such an extent that sometimes fewer than 100 customers would grace its doors.

On the rare nights that the lads did go to Springs, the bus journey

was still an experience like no other. Sing-a-longs, always orches-
trated by the Rams, were almost a certainty on the way from Oldcastle
to Springs. And sometimes the return journey was just as much fun.
One night after the disco ended, the lads hopped onto their waiting
mini-bus. It was a small vehicle with just two facing rows of seats
in the back, but there was also room for two or three passengers in
the front beside the driver. It was like having your own private bus,
and the lads revelled in singing and messing without having to worry
about there being any other passengers onboard who might not care
for such behaviour. Just as the bus was about to leave Springs, two
strangers hopped on. One sat beside the Rams and the other directly
opposite him.

Somewhere between the Springs and Ballyjamesduff, the singing started. And of course it was none other than Munterconnaught's
greatest singing sensation, the Rams, who kicked things off. As
usual, the first song of choice was *The Rattlin' Bog*. It's a traditional
Irish song, the words of which vary slightly from county to county.
Rams had learned a version of the song from Mark McGovern many
years earlier when they, along with Goosey and Stano, were going
from house to house in Munterconnaught as the wren boys on Saint
Stephen's day. Every time someone sang *The Rattlin' Bog*—whether
it be in a pub, at a house party or indeed in a mini-bus—everyone
present was encouraged to join in on the chorus.

'O-ro the rattlin' bog,
A way down in the valley-o.
O-ro the rattlin' bog,
A way down in the valley-o.'

The added beauty of *'The Rattlin' Bog'* lies in its verses, which get
longer and are sung faster as the song progresses. Rams had just completed the introductory chorus and had started on the first verse when
the stranger sitting opposite him erupted.

'Shut the fuck up with that shite or I'll fuckin' swing for ya,' he said
aggressively.

Rams was never one to look for a fight but, at the same time, he didn't take shit from anyone, least of all some stranger who had been fortunate enough to be given a seat on a mini-bus that had been specifically ordered by the Rams and his friends.

'You and whose army?' Rams retorted. 'We do this all the time so, if you don't like it, tough. Nobody asked ya to get on this bus.'

And then the Rams continued where he'd left off. As the bus meandered through quiet country roads, he began flying through the verses, the words flowing from his mouth at an admirable pace.

'... *And the tree on the branch,*
And the branch on the tree,
And the tree on the bog,
A way down in the valley-o.'

While catching a breath, Rams momentarily looked out the bus window at the dark surroundings that were but mile after mile of trees and hedges. The stranger, availing of this opportunistic opening, lunged at the loud singer. He didn't manage to get too far though. Stano, who was sitting beside the aggressor, quickly grabbed him and threw him back into the seat, warning him to stay seated and behave himself. The stranger's friend also attempted to keep the peace and spoke to him in an attempt to calm him down. But it was to no avail. Seconds later he again lunged at the Rams, and this time all hell broke loose.

As Rams sprung to his feet to defend himself, he accidentally hit the light switch, plunging the bus into sheer blackness and chaos. All the lads in the back immediately found themselves involved in a fistfight—Rams and his five friends against the two strangers. The balance would have been a little uneven where it not that it was impossible to see anything in the dark and, therefore, random and wild punches became the order of the day.

As the fighting rocked the bus, the driver slammed on the brakes and flung open the sliding door at the back of the vehicle. With everyone still oblivious to his presence, a stray elbow suddenly hit him in the mouth. The resultant roar brought the fight to a standstill, and then each of the lads scrambled to find a seat in the darkness before the inevitable lecture began.

'I'm not driving this bus any further. Yas are a pack of animals, the lot of ya. We'll just stay here now for as long as it takes for yas to learn some fuckin' manners,' the driver screamed while holding his swollen face.

The lads all sat in silence for several minutes before the driver agreed to journey onwards. He deserved a holiday after enduring such a stressful and physical night's work, but it was some of the lads in the back of the bus who would soon be taking one, and there was but one place on Earth big enough to contain them.

Chapter 31

NEW YORK, NEW YORK

NEW YORK. Surely the most recognisable city in the world, its iconic landmarks and storied history had always appealed to the Rams. It represented a completely opposite reality to the one he had known growing up. A heaving city with eight million residents seemed like an impossibility to a young boy growing up in a rural community that consisted of a sprinkling of houses dotted throughout a gloriously green countryside.

Rams's older sister, Vanessa, and her boyfriend, Klaas, lived in Germany and, after visiting them in April 2001, the Rams felt the need to do more travelling and see more of the world. And where bigger or better than New York City? Rams was delighted when Goosey, Stano and Mara agreed to go with him, and he set about booking flights and accommodation for an eight-night holiday in October.

Six weeks before the lads were due to fly to New York, the unimaginable happened. It was 11 September, and Rams had just returned from lunch and was sitting at his desk at work. A few minutes later he was standing in the reception watching the big television screen with a number of his colleagues and barely comprehending what was happening before his eyes. Less than an hour earlier, a pair of hijacked passenger jets had crashed into the World Trade Center's Twin Towers. Then, just after arriving at the reception, Rams witnessed the South Tower collapse live—almost in slow motion—as the entire world looked on. The North Tower fell shortly thereafter and, in the days that followed, the residents of New York tried to come to terms with their city's darkest hour.

There was little doubt that terrorists—namely the Al-Qaeda—were behind the atrocious attacks, but many Americans wanted to know whether the attacks could have been prevented or even predicted. In the aftermath of 11 September, an email quoting Nostradamus began circulating worldwide. It seemed to suggest that the prophet had predicted the catastrophe.

'In the City of God, there will be a great thunder,
Two brothers torn apart by chaos,
While the fortress endures,
The great leader will succumb,
The third big war will begin when the big city is burning.'

After Rams forwarded the email to a group of friends, Goosey replied almost immediately with his own unique interpretation.

'Sure 'tis obvious what that Nostradamus eejit is saying. He's talking about the Cavan U14 Rionn-A final of '92, a battle between Munterconnaught and Maghera. Twas on in Breffni in Cavan town (City of God) and there was a bit of an argie bargie and I was involved. A brother of mine, a pacifist, was trying to hold me back but we ended up scrapping (Two brothers torn apart). Then our great leader (you know, the 'beating heart of the club' type) lost the plot and lamped an opposing selector, but still the fortress of the Munterconnaught goals endured. A mass brawl broke out later in the town (sorry, city) when the Maghera boys tried to fire bomb the chipper we were loitering around. So there's no cause for panic folks; everyone survived that fateful night.'

In its own way, Goosey's tongue-in-cheek interpretation showed how easily vague terms can be applied to fit any event. And it soon emerged that a student in Canada had in fact written the quatrain in 1997 as part of an essay on Nostradamus, which attempted to prove that point. In the wake of 9/11, an unknown scribe added the final line to add legitimacy and meaning to the hoax email, thus fooling many unsuspecting Americans.

Six weeks later Rams, Stano and Mara arrived at Dublin Airport. After clearing the security checks without any problems, they had to fill in customs and immigration forms. Rams had packed a six-pack of crisps in his luggage. Many of his fussy eating habits from childhood had carried through to adulthood, and the crisps would be his lifeline if a potato famine occurred during his time in America. As Rams scanned the forms, he noticed a question asking whether or not he was carrying food amongst his luggage. He was unsure how to answer the question but decided that even though crisps probably wouldn't be classed as food under these circumstances, he would tick the 'yes' box and deal with the consequences afterwards.

Upon completion of the forms, a short interrogation by customs and immigration officials was warranted before the lads could board the plane. Rams stepped up to the booth and began answering with ease the myriad of questions coming his way. Then came the big one.

'What food are you carrying in your luggage, sir?' asked the American official in a heavily-accented voice.

Rams suddenly realised that due to the official's nationality he probably wouldn't be familiar with the Irish meaning of the word crisps. Crisps are known as chips in America while chips—as referred to in Ireland—correlate with French fries across the Atlantic. Rams knew this so all he had to do was mention that he had six bags of chips in his luggage, and everything would be okay. Unfortunately, he drew a blank and seemed unable to get the word crisps out of his mind. He turned quickly to Stano for some assistance.

'What do they call crisps in America?'

Stano didn't give it a second thought. He just said the first thing that came into his head.

'Tayto,' he said, looking rather pleased with himself for coming to Rams's rescue.

Tayto is an Irish crisps and popcorn manufacturer, and the name is almost synonymous with any sort of crisps in Ireland, regardless of brand. Despite the popularity of the brand, its main market lies in its home country, so the chances were that the American customs official had never heard the word Tayto before.

But he had heard enough all the same. As Rams shook his head in disbelief at Stano's reply, the official gave him the green light to proceed. He was obviously satisfied that there was nothing untoward about these two Irish lads. They seemed too stupid to be terrorists. Mara caught up with the lads a few moments later.

'John Joe was a bit nosey for my liking,' he remarked.

Mara referred to pretty much everyone as John Joe. It saved trying to remember names and, although strangers would look suspiciously at him when he'd ask them, 'What's your name John Joe?', his friends were used to it and sure it wasn't really any worse than being addressed as 'Merchant' or 'Horse'.

It was a glorious October afternoon when the lads arrived at JFK Airport. They wasted little time in hailing a taxi from outside the terminal building to New York's East Village where the Rams had booked an apartment for the duration of their stay. After collecting the keys from the owner, the lads took a look around the apartment while waiting for Goosey. There was a large and nicely-furnished sitting room, small kitchen, bathroom and two bedrooms. Rams took the double room, and Stano and Mara threw their luggage into the twin room. A couch in the sitting room, which folded out as a large bed, would accommodate the fourth tenant. And just where was Goosey?

He was due to arrive in New York shortly after his friends, and had told them to leave the apartment after settling in, turn right after leaving the building and start walking, and he'd meet them in the nearest bar. That plan was sound in theory but after a few minutes' walking the lads still hadn't come across a single bar. They soon arrived at a crossroads and discovered they now had the opposite problem. There were bars to the left and bars to the right. Rams suggested having a quick pint in the nearest bar left of the junction and then returning to the apartment to wait for Goosey. After quickly quenching their thirst, the lads started walking towards the apartment and were fortunate to meet Goosey on the street en route. He had only just arrived. Now the fellowship was complete, and it was time to let the good times roll.

Over the next week the lads partied hard by night and took in all manner of tourist attractions by day. Walking through lower Manhattan for the first time was an eye-opener for the Rams. He was expecting tall buildings for sure but the sheer scale and height of the skyscrapers blew him away. The food too was a far cry from the small-scale portions he was accustomed to in Ireland. Plates were piled high with food, and steak seemed to be served with everything—steak with breakfast, steak with lunch, steak with dinner. You couldn't order an ice cream without half a cow being lobbed on top of it.

East Village turned out to be a good area to stay in because it gave the lads a better idea of what living in New York was like in comparison to what some fancy hotel would. The bars were small and dingy, and an abundance of homeless beggars walked the streets at night, but it was still a pleasant neighbourhood in which to wander. Rams noticed there were a few fortune tellers located close to the apartment. He didn't particularly believe any of that 'mumbo jumbo' but, with just a few hours remaining before returning to Ireland, he decided to waste a few dollars by trying something new.

Goosey tried to accompany the Rams through the door of the dreary premises, but the fortune teller quickly blocked his path, telling him, 'only one customer at a time.'

'It's okay. I'm his spiritual adviser,' Goosey lamented. But the attempt at humour was wasted on the strange woman, and she ushered the unwanted adviser out the door. Rams briefly scanned his surroundings. The dark room appeared to be connected to a flat by a narrow doorway. The door was ajar, and he could see a sitting room in the background.

'*I suppose that's one way of working from home,*' he thought.

The fortune teller obviously wasn't too good at her job because she failed to prophesise Rams point blankly refusing to pay the outlandish fees she was quoting for a reading. But she continued negotiating, nonetheless, until Rams asked her, 'What can I get for five dollars?'

A forehead reading was the not so obvious answer. This apparently would equate to a personality reading whereby the amazingly talented fortune teller would reveal loads of facts about the Rams's multi-faceted personality; and all by just staring intently at his forehead.

Rams soon sussed out the tricks of the dodgy woman's trade. She would ask him a vague question such as, 'What happened four years ago?' She would then attempt to use the answer as a catalyst for her ambiguous ramblings before asking another ridiculous question like, 'Who is Kristin or Kayla?'

The Rams couldn't recall the events of the previous night, never mind what happened four years previously. And he didn't know a Kristin or Kayla either.

'This psychic should at least research Irish names before horsin' out this shite,' he thought, knowing that there was no danger of his mind being read.

'There's someone really bad in your life; maybe a John or a Joe,' said the psychic, hoping for a reaction from the Rams so she would have something to latch onto. But his face was giving nothing away, so she continued. 'You need to rid this person from your life because they are no good.' She then attempted to sell Rams a selection of candles, the burning of which would remove the bad karma surrounding him and, at 30 dollars a candle, the bad karma wouldn't be the only thing disappearing. Fortunately, Rams somehow managed to make it back to the lads with his wallet intact.

Although the fortune teller had correctly assessed certain aspects of Rams's personality, she had thrown enough shit at the wall so that some of it was bound to stick and, therefore, Rams remained unconvinced of her clairvoyant powers.

'Well, lads. Ya should have heard the stuff yer wan was coming out with. She said there's a John or Joe holding me back in life, and I need to get shot of them. Sure I don't know any Johns well, and the only Joe I know is Fingering Joe. That's not even his real name. And besides, I haven't seen him in years.'

'John or Joe,' Stano pondered.

'John Joe,' Mara chipped in, seemingly putting the pieces of the puzzle together.

'You're right,' Rams exclaimed. 'John Joe. It makes sense now. She didn't see John or Joe, but the two together—John Joe. Sure John Joe is everyone I know. So what she's really saying is that everyone in my life is a wanker.'

The true meaning of Madam Bullshit's ravings would have to be debated another day because the lads had just enough time to take a quick jaunt into central Manhattan to pick up a few presents and souvenirs before a flight home beckoned. Following the brief shopping spree, Rams and Goosey still had a few dollars burning a hole in their wallets, but it was time to flag down a taxi to the airport. Rams hadn't yet bought anything for his father, and the only things close by that screamed, 'I've been to New York', were the fake Rolexes and other cheap watches being sold in abundance by the nearby street traders. Rams picked up a Rolex and a 'normal' watch for about 20 dollars, and Goosey also helped himself to a Rolex.

Ten minutes later the lads were driving towards the airport in a taxi. The end of the holiday was nigh, and Rams was reflecting on what had been a thoroughly enjoyable experience. He knew it was only a matter of time before he'd return to America and the Big Apple, and that time couldn't come quick enough.

'What time is it now, Goosey?' asked Stano, breaking the silence.

'I don't fuckin' believe it,' Goosey bawled. 'My watch has stopped.'

'Ya just can't get the Rolexes these days,' remarked the Rams.

Everyone laughed at Goosey's misfortune, and even the taxi driver broke a smile as he sped along the motorway towards JFK Airport.

Chapter 32

MUNTERCONNAUGHT'S OTHER SONS

ALTHOUGH THE Rams had been living in Dublin for a few years and had formed numerous close friendships in the city, his ties with many of Munterconnaught's sons were stronger than ever. Dowd may have been at the other side of the world, and Goosey remained in London, but some of Rams's other old school friends were now either living in Dublin or visiting the city on a semi-regular basis.

Rams had barely clapped eyes on Mark McGovern or Pauric Tighe since leaving primary school over a decade earlier. McGovern, who had recently rediscovered the joys of alcohol after a seven-year hiatus, began regularly socialising with Stano, and the pair would often meet the Rams in Dublin for a weekend of drinking and mayhem. Pauric, still a close friend of McGovern's since primary school, would also meet the lads when he could. And when Pauric had to work a late shift in the pub he was managing in Phibsboro, his brother, Eugene, would take his place. Eugene was four years Pauric's junior and was every bit the lunatic his brother was. The Tighe brothers looked and acted alike and, whether drunk or sober, they were great fun to be around.

One of the first times Rams went drinking with the Tighes, they ended up in a trendy Dublin club, which was renowned for its posh clientele. Beautiful women adorned every corner of the club but, for many of them, this beauty was only skin-deep. They were clearly in love with themselves as evidenced by their spending one half of the night looking at themselves in the wall-length mirrors, which were everywhere, and the other half speaking in exaggerated fake accents about, 'Daddy's yacht', and how, 'My credit card is sooo maxed out.'

Pauric just couldn't resist. It was time to bring these people down a peg or two using typically unorthodox Munterconnaught humour. Sliding up beside a girl at the bar, he began making small talk and, predictably, his intended victim attempted to ignore him while sticking her nose so far up in the air that she was in danger of injuring herself.

'Do you know what?' asked Pauric while shifting his gaze towards her shapely posterior.

'What?' she asked indignantly.

'Ya have an arse like a 10 year old boy,' he said, somehow keeping a straight face.

Pauric's friends exploded in laughter as 'Little Miss Attitude' fled the bar at an alarming speed, and he wondered out loud why she couldn't take a compliment. Yes, Pauric was still as bold as the Rams remembered him to be all those years earlier in primary school.

McGovern hadn't changed much either. He was still a hardy bastard and, although he was only of average height and slightly stocky build, his Samson-esque strength had multiplied 20-fold over the years. Therefore, he had transformed from a hardy bastard into THE hardest bastard in the country. A friendly punch on the shoulder from McGovern was enough to cause his friends to grimace in pain. And God help anyone he took a disliking to.

McGovern was also one of the few people who cursed more than the Rams, and he was particularly fond of using the word 'cunt' in almost every sentence.

'Ho ho, ya cunt ya,' was his standard greeting any time the Rams called him on his mobile.

Despite McGovern's hard-as-nails exterior, Rams soon discovered that, more than almost anyone else he knew, McGovern truly seemed to have his priorities in life properly balanced. He worked hard to make a living, but he valued family and friends more than anything, and was generous almost to a fault. He was also extremely funny, both through his actions and his words. At the first sign of trouble on a night out, McGovern would wade in with the two fists and, whether there were two, three or a half dozen troublemakers, it was guaranteed he would emerge victorious and unscathed, a mass of crumbling bodies lying in his wake.

Watching McGovern in action was funny enough, but listening to him regaling the events of a beating provided even more entertainment. He would always start a story by mentioning that he hadn't been in a fight in years, and one might assume from this that he must have been really provoked to lose his temper. The funny thing was that it usually took no more than a dirty look for McGovern to unleash the fists, or sledgehammers as some people called them.

'Sure I haven't been in a row in over three years, but this lad spilt my pint. Well, I hit the cunt a box, and bejaysis his head nearly came clean off.'

Anytime McGovern visited Dublin, a long weekend of drinking was undoubtedly in store. Rams loved partying with McGovern, but he soon realised that these gargantuan sessions couldn't continue for much longer. Rams usually socialised with some of his work colleagues mid-week, and then the weekend would herald the arrival of McGovern, Stano, the Tighe brothers and whoever else was around. Drinking five nights a week mightn't be unusual for many of Ireland's youthful population, but Rams was living beyond his means and was now spending more money each month than he was earning.

McGovern also spent several weekends in London on the lash with Goosey. He told the Rams that he was going to move there permanently, but Rams had his doubts. McGovern had lived his whole life in Munterconnaught and was doing very well for himself as a builder. Even when he began a serious relationship with a girl in London, Rams's doubts persisted.

When Goosey landed in Dublin one weekend on the same night that McGovern, Stano and Eugene Tighe were in town, Rams knew that a chaotic few days were on the cards. A heavy night's drinking on Friday was followed by a trip home to Munterconnaught and a night out in Oldcastle on the Saturday. By Sunday morning the Rams was almost on bended knees but, nonetheless, he joined Goosey and McGovern in Boylan's for the hair of the dog.

Any time Rams was in Cavan for the weekend, he would always return to Dublin on a Sunday evening via the 8.30pm bus from Virginia. On this particular Sunday he arrived home from Boylan's at 6.30pm, and was mouldy drunk. After devouring a reheated Sunday dinner, he went straight to bed, telling his parents to wake him up in time to catch the bus to Dublin.

12 hours later the Rams awoke with a start. After realising that it was Monday morning and he had to be at work in two and a half hours, he jumped out of bed and began packing a bag. Apparently his parents had no luck waking him the previous evening and, therefore, had been forced to let him sleep off the effects of three days' solid drinking.

Somehow Rams managed to get to work in Dublin on time and, although it felt like the day would never end, he eventually returned to his apartment, tired and hoping that he wouldn't see McGovern or any of the Tighes again for a long time.

Within two hours the intercom phone rang. Rams shuffled into the hallway and wearily picked up the receiver.

'Ho ho, ya cunt ya,' roared the instantly recognisable voice.

'Ah for fuck sake,' thought the Rams. *'What the hell is he doing back in Dublin?'*

'What are ya at?' said a barely comprehensible McGovern. He had obviously been drinking all day, and he wasn't alone. 'Eugene's here with me. Come on, we're going for beer.'

'Yas may go without me,' said the Rams. 'There's no way I'm going out tonight.'

'Get down here ya cunt ya or I'll knock your fuckin' door in and drag ya out,' was the reply.

Rams knew better than to argue with McGovern. And he was about 99 percent sure that his would-be visitor was about 10 seconds away from removing the front door of the building from its hinges.

'Hold on. I'll be down in a second,' he said reluctantly.

McGovern and Eugene were kicking the shite out of a waste bin when Rams met them outside the apartment block. They could hardly have been any drunker but were still gagging for more alcohol. The Rams promptly decided to bring them to his local pub, where he planned on having no more than two or three pints before sneaking home at the first available opportunity.

Rams soon learned that Goosey and McGovern had gone to Dublin the previous evening while he was out for the count in Virginia. Goosey's flight to London had been due to depart on Monday morning, and it would have been almost rude had McGovern not accompanied him to Dublin for one final farewell hooley. The two lads were still fairly polluted from their Boylan's session when they arrived in Dublin and met Eugene in Phibsboro to continue the drinking spree in a nearby pub.

As the night progressed, Goosey and McGovern reached new levels of drunkenness, and Eugene tried his best to play catch-up with them. Shortly before closing time, Goosey mistakenly picked up a stranger's pint and, assuming it to be his own, began guzzling it with enthusiasm. The owner of the pint didn't see the funny side of the situation, and threw a punch in Goosey's direction. McGovern immediately went into attack mode and, with one of his sledgehammers, sent the stranger *Matrix*-style into the air. Meanwhile Eugene was talking to a girl at the other side of the pub.

'Aren't those your friends over there?' she asked.

Eugene looked across the room and quickly realised it was time to leave. Goosey was gulping down the remnants of a pint of lager and, to his right, McGovern was throwing punches at anyone who dared look in his direction. The bodies were quickly piling up, and the bar manager appeared to be calling the cops on the nearby phone.

The following night in Ram's local, McGovern was beaming with pride as he regurgitated his adventures from Phibsboro.

'Well I hit the cunt a box, and bejaysis I lifted him six feet off the floor. And the eyes rolling in his head before he hit the ground.'

McGovern's story was hilarious the first time he told it but, just as he was about to repeat it for a third time, two Dubliners saved the day by sitting beside the lads. One of them, a pretty blonde haired girl, asked McGovern for a lighter, and he began a conversation with her about London and how he was going to move there soon. As McGovern rambled on, Rams and Eugene became transfixed—for all the wrong reasons—with the blonde girl's friend.

'Rams, is that a man or a woman?' shouted Eugene in a drunken whisper.

'I'm not sure, Horse,' Rams replied. 'She's either a really masculine woman or he's a really feminine man. Either way, she or he is what I'd call an "Itsy".'

An Itsy is a person who cannot, at first glance, be easily identified as either male or female. And the blonde girl's friend certainly fitted the bill. Short hair but a very feminine face suggested that it could a woman. But without a positive ID on a pair of breasts or anything else synonymous with the fairer sex, Rams's jury was still out.

McGovern, however, soon delivered a verdict.

'And what's your name, love?' he asked the Itsy.

The reply took McGovern completely by surprise. He had assumed he was speaking to a woman, but the gruff voice that emerged from the hitherto silent Itsy suggested otherwise. Of course the actual words spoken also served as a bit of a clue.

'My name is Michael.'

McGovern took a second to digest what he had just heard and then, with a disgusted expression devouring his face, he turned to face the Rams.

'Ah Jaysis, it's a man,' he bawled, his eyes almost popping out of his head in shock.

Michael didn't seem overjoyed with the outburst. Fortunately, his blonde girlfriend felt otherwise. In fact she looked mildly amused, not only by McGovern's outburst but also by Rams and Eugene who were now in tears with the laughter.

A few weeks later McGovern, true to his word, moved to London. And of course this presented Rams with the perfect excuse to visit the city that summer for the first time in two years.

The Rams landed in Manchester on a Thursday evening in August 2002. He had decided to spend a night there prior to catching a train to London the following day. Rams's good friend, Rob, lived in Manchester and would be joining him on the trip to London.

Rob had studied Multimedia with the Rams in Waterford, and the pair had also attended college together in Dublin for a year before Rob moved to Manchester in January 2000. They remained good friends and, any time Rob returned to his hometown of Dublin, he and the Rams would head out on the rip in Temple Bar.

With the possible exception of Stano, Rob was peerless when it came to making the Rams laugh. He was extremely witty and a rather good impressionist. He could do a great impression of Christy Brown or, to be precise, a great impression of Daniel Day Lewis doing a great impression of Christy Brown. Rams did a good Christy impression himself although he knew that Rob's efforts were far superior. The pair would often have 'Christy Competitions' in the pub, which would involve conversing 'in character'. Rams's efforts would garner a few chuckles, but Rob always stole the show, a long trail of dribble hanging from his chin often serving as the clincher.

Rob's obligatory nickname was Lord Doctor Francis Rupert Barrett. It was perhaps the most absurd moniker the Rams had ever conceived; yet it made perfect sense in his unique mind. Rob had grown up in Sutton, one of Dublin's plusher suburbs. Therefore, Rams believed Rob should have a title or two before his name; hence Lord and Doctor. Rupert was 'short' for Rob, and the Francis and Barrett parts of the name were shared with an Irish traveller who had represented Ireland in the Olympics some years earlier. And so Rob's nickname supposedly represented two opposites of Irish society and suggested that he was a true man of the people.

After enjoying a night out in Manchester, Rams and Rob made their way to London on Friday afternoon. Goosey, who was now living with a bunch of people on Marylebone Road, had offered to put the lads up for the weekend. It wasn't just Goosey and his flatmates, however, who greeted the pair when they arrived. A man severely lacking in the shame department had returned from his Australian and round-the-world adventures, and the timing couldn't have been any better.

Rams knew Dowd was due back in London sometime in August, and he had emailed the shameless one a few weeks earlier to see if he would be there in time for his and Rob's visit. But an unusually evasive response from Dowd had caused Rams to think that just maybe Goosey and McGovern wouldn't be the only Munterconnaught men to meet him in London that weekend. Nonetheless, Rams was still pleasantly surprised when Dowd appeared from nowhere in the flat, his right hand outstretched for a heart-felt handshake.

A severe lack of cows in Dowd's diet for a few weeks while returning to London via India had caused him to lose some weight but, other than that, he was in fantastic form and eager to share some stories from his extensive trip. After pausing for a brief moment, he turned to the Rams.

'What are ya doing for Paddy's Day?' he asked.

Rams hadn't anything planned for the near future other than meeting McGovern at some stage over the weekend for a few pints. And Saint Patrick's Day was over seven months away, so obviously he hadn't given it any thought.

'Nothing. Why?'

'What would ye say to a trip to New York?'

Chapter 33

BACK TO NEW YORK

'HOLD ON there. I have a lad here who wants to talk to ya,' screamed McGovern. It was about 3 o'clock in the morning. Goosey had been fast asleep seconds prior to the phone ringing. Now, with his eyes still half-closed, he could hear loud music in the background and McGovern passing his mobile to one of his companions.

'Come here,' said the stranger. 'Book me up on that fuckin' trip, will ya?'

'Yeah, no bother,' said Goosey, raising his eyes towards Heaven before hanging up and switching his mobile off. This wasn't the first late-night phone call from one of McGovern's friends. Numbers for the Saint Patrick's Day trip had recently been spiralling out of control, with the headcount rising each week as various people requested to be part of what would undoubtedly be an outrageous session. By the time March 2003 rolled round, over a dozen men were booked onto the holiday, which had now been scaled up to include more than New York. Although McGovern couldn't make the trip, Munterconnaught was well represented by Rams, Goosey, Dowd and Trevor Geraghty. Boo Boo flew the flag for Oldcastle, and the rest of the crew were mainly Irish ex-pats living in London.

Rams arrived alone in Boston on Friday 14 March. The rest of the gang would join him a day later after spending two nights in Reykjavik. A beautiful afternoon welcomed the Rams back to America; melting snow along the roads being the only indication that a big freeze had recently gripped the city. The All-Irishman, Big Ron, had moved to Boston the previous year, so the lads had added the city to their travel itinerary in order to catch up with him and take in all that Boston had to offer.

After staying the night at Ron's house in the charming neighbourhood of Dorchester, Rams gathered himself together on Saturday afternoon and made his way to the Hilton Boston Back Bay Hotel, where he and the remainder of the lads were booked in for a night. Predictably much drinking, reminiscing and general mayhem ensued throughout the evening and into the early hours of the morning. That night, however, would only serve as a warm-up. New York beckoned and, with it, the prospect of the biggest Paddy's Day hooley any of the lads had ever witnessed.

A comfortable train journey from Boston brought the lads to New York's Penn Station in about three hours. From there, it was only a short walk to Hotel Pennsylvania on 7th Avenue. Although not the plushest of establishments, the hotel managed to impress due to its enormous size; 1,700 rooms made it one of the largest hotels in New York and undoubtedly one of the largest buildings of any kind that most members of the group had ever stepped foot in.

With Paddy's Day but a few hours away, the lads planned on having a few quiet pints in a nearby bar and retiring early in anticipation of what would be an all-day drinking marathon the following day. Of course the few quiet pints gave way to more somewhat louder pints, and most of the lads were fairly tipsy as they barged out of the bar in search of a taxi to the next drinking emporium.

A moustached man in his late fifties was sweeping the pavement outside the bar when the Rams confronted him, camera in hand. Rams and Dowd were renowned for gathering huge numbers of strangers together in bars for group photos. It was never too difficult to recruit eager volunteers. Rams, however, didn't just rely on group photos for his holiday snaps. Individuals doing unusual things were also ripe for snapping, and a man sweeping a footpath in the middle of the night certainly fitted this criteria. That he was wearing an expensive suit further encouraged Rams to unintentionally annoy him.

'Can I get a photo with ya, Merchant?' asked the Rams, passing his camera to Trevor.

'No, No,' said the sweeper, turning his back to the Rams while nodding his head in indignation.

Nobody had ever turned down an invitation to have their photo taken with the Rams and, as a result, he wasn't sure how to react.

'Ah come on. Sure it's only a wee photo,' he said, putting his arm around the stranger who again turned his back to Rams and began walking away. Then, in a moment of madness and without warning, the Rams jumped onto the sweeper's back and roared at Trevor to, 'Take the photo.'

Trevor duly obliged and a bright flash accompanied a click from the camera as the sweeper's legs almost buckled under Rams's weight. Rams then dismounted and ran over to Trevor to see if he had managed to capture the moment on film. Then, after briefly composing himself, the sweeper marched over to the Rams and demanded an explanation for what had just happened.

'Sorry there, man. I just wanted to get a photo,' said the Rams half-jokingly. Eventually the sweeper calmed down and returned to where he had been working in peace moments earlier. Rams should have been thankful that the cops hadn't been called, but instead he rather stupidly began bragging about the incident to some of the other lads who had just stumbled out of the bar.

This deplorable act obviously incensed the sweeper, and he darted over to the Rams, removed a wallet from his pocket and flashed a cop badge at the smart ass who suddenly wasn't feeling so smart any more.

Rams eventually talked his way out of the situation once again, this time playing the 'thick Irish man' card and pretending that it was his first night in a foreign country and he didn't know any better. After being nearly carted off to jail, he couldn't help but reflect on the incident as he and the lads made their way to another bar.

'What the fuck were the chances that a lad sweeping the footpath would be an undercover cop?' he wondered aloud. 'Well that sure brings a new meaning to the expression, "On the pig's back".'

Rams, Goosey and Boo Boo started Paddy's Day with a big fry-up in Queens. They had attempted to watch the parade in Manhattan an hour earlier but the enormity of the crowds gathered on every street quickly turned their thoughts to food and the prospect of a quiet pint before the bars became thronged. A few hours later the bars in Queens were still pretty empty, so the three lads—along with the remainder of the gang—headed back to Manhattan.

Paddy's Day in New York is something that everyone should experience at least once. It seemed like an army dressed in green had taken over the city, and everyone the Rams encountered was either Irish or claiming to be Irish. Rams couldn't recall a day when he'd spoken to more people in such a relaxed and carefree environment. As the lads sauntered down a random street in Lower Manhattan in the middle of the afternoon, they bumped into Eugene Tighe who was in New York for a week with his sister, Leona, and a group of her friends. Rams had been trying to contact Eugene at his hotel since arriving in New York, but to no avail. And then, of all the bars in all the streets in New York, the two happened to meet completely by accident. After the obligatory reference to what a small world it really is, Eugene joined the lads for a few pints. The banter was mighty, and many tales were told, some of which centred on Oldcastle's and Munterconnaught's colourful characters.

'Did ya hear the latest about Paddy Joe McCarthy?' asked the Rams, referring to one of Oldcastle's renowned oddballs.

'No. What's he at this weather?' returned Goosey.

'Well apparently he's living in a small village in Donegal these days. But you'll never guess what he did the other week.'

'What did he do?' asked Eugene impatiently.

'Well,' said the Rams before taking a deep breath. 'He showed up at his local grocery shop wearing a wrestling t-shirt and a balaclava. He then held a pen-knife to the cashier and demanded the contents of the till.'

'You're joking,' laughed Eugene.

'No. It gets better,' continued Rams. 'He then returned to the shop the very same afternoon, minus the balaclava and pen-knife, but still wearing the exact same clothes, including the unmistakable wrestling t-shirt. Supposedly he reckoned the shopkeeper wouldn't think him stupid enough to return to the scene of the crime on the same day it was committed. Luckily for him, his stupidity turned out to be his best defence and was the only thing that prevented him from going to jail when he went before the courts.'

'Poor old Paddy Joe,' said Dowd, shaking his head.

Rams loved nothing more than having a few pints with old friends while reminiscing about times past and planning ahead for times yet to come. And Paddy's Day was proving to be the perfect time to do just that and to meet loads of new, friendly people. Alas, the moment was short-lived and the next morning many of the lads, including Goosey and Dowd, were either London-bound or catching flights to other parts of America.

Fortunately, Trevor, Boo Boo and four of the London-based contingent were staying in New York for another two nights. Ron and his Boston-based Irish friend, who had both travelled to New York for the festivities, decided to stay just one more night in Hotel Penn. But with everyone wrecked after the excessiveness of Paddy's Day, Tuesday night in Manhattan proved to be a very sedate affair.

The City That Never Sleeps was still in a comatose state on Wednesday night, but that wasn't going to prevent Rams from enjoying his last few hours there before returning to Boston. Only Eugene and a lad named John summoned enough energy to join the Rams for a few pints, although finding a lively venue was to prove difficult.

While drinking in one almost derelict bar, the lads asked the barman for the names of a few decent watering holes. Armed with this new information, they hit the streets in good spirits but soon ended up hopelessly lost near Times Square. As they waited for the lights to turn green at a pedestrian crossing, Rams spotted a black man across the street. He appeared to be rather animated for some reason and was waving and shouting in an attempt to catch the lads' attention. His shoddy clothes suggested that he was homeless, and the time spent on the streets had obviously given him the skills necessary to

spot tourists from a distance. Of course the strong Irish accents emanating from the three lads offered a small clue that they weren't New
Yorkers.

Watching the man approach, Rams immediately likened him to
Eddie Murphy's character in the movie *Trading Places*. Leroy, as he
was called, had an extraordinarily friendly, loud and confident personality, which he utilised to full effect so that it was nearly impossible
for innocent tourists to tell him to get lost.

'Where are you guys going?' he asked.

Eugene showed him a piece of paper with the name of a bar
scrawled on it.

'No problem. Follow me,' said Leroy.

Rams tried to protest, but Leroy wasn't one for negotiating, and
he began marching up the street, arms waving erratically at his sides.
Meanwhile Eugene walked behind him and tried his best to replicate
the unusual walk. Leroy was oblivious to what was going on behind
his back and he never let up talking for a second, mostly just repeating
himself again and again.

'I'll take you there, no problem. I'll take you right to the door,' he
said.

'Well maybe not just right to the door,' John interjected. 'We want
to get in.'

Rams burst out laughing. He could almost picture the scene in his
head—he and the lads arriving at one of the few busy bars in town,
only to be denied entry because there was a homeless person in their
company.

Leroy didn't bat an eyelid at the remark and, true to his word,
brought the lads to their destination in double quick time. Now it was
time to collect his fee.

'Hey, cut a man a bit of plak,' he hollered. 'A man can't sleep another night standin' up in the subway. And ya gotta sleep standin' up
cos if ya sit down they'll move ya along. So show a man a bit of
plak.'

The lads all dug deep. If nothing else, Leroy had been more entertaining than the average taxi driver, so he deserved a premium rate.

Once Leroy had been paid and after getting past the bouncers, Rams realised that it just wasn't his night. Another near-empty bar! Two beautiful women near the entrance momentarily distracted the lads, but unfortunately they finished their drinks and left the bar moments later, leaving the lads stuck looking at each other once again. John decided to head back to the hotel early, but Rams and Eugene weren't prepared to surrender the cause just yet, and they wandered down the street and into the next bar they happened upon.

The second bar wasn't any better than the first, with only five or six customers staring gloomily at half-empty glasses. No sooner had Rams and Eugene stepped into the premises, however, than they noticed the two gorgeous girls from the previous bar. They were seated at the side of the bar counter, one of them with her back to the bar and the other sitting adjacent to her. Rams had seldom seen two women as beautiful as this pair. They were both very tall, with long slender legs, immaculate blonde hair and piercing blue eyes. Rams and Eugene knew they wouldn't stand a chance with the beauties, but that didn't prevent Munterconnaught's would-be Lotharios from debating amongst themselves over which of the two girls was checking them out.

Then two English men joined the lads at the bar. After a bit of small talk, the conversation inevitably turned to the stunning blondes sitting in the corner. Rams and Eugene light-heartedly suggested that they had been on the verge of scoring the pair until the two Brits showed up to cramp their style.

'I bet you boys couldn't chat those girls up for more than a minute,' said Alan, the more outspoken of the Brits.

'Make it five minutes and we have a deal,' said an over-cocky Rams.

After deciding that the losers of the wager would have to buy the winners a drink of their choosing, Rams and Eugene strode confidently over to the blondes and sat down beside them.

'Well, ladies. How are yas getting on?' began Eugene, the wide smile on his face suggesting that he had already won the bet.

'We're just hanging out,' replied one of the girls in a strong New

York accent.

That's as far as the conversation went. The barman suddenly rushed over and didn't mix his words in conveying to the lads that their company was neither required nor desired.

'Guys, move away from there now,' he said sternly.

Rams hadn't even been afforded the opportunity to say a single word to either of the women, but the expression on the barman's face ensured that Rams's first words to them—as he picked up his beer from the table—were regretful goodbyes.

'See yas later, girls,' he said reluctantly as he and Eugene returned crestfallen to the bar counter. The two Brits were smiling from ear to ear, delighted that the lads had barely managed to spend 30 seconds in the company of the two stunners.

As the Brits enjoyed their carefully chosen and expensive cocktails, Rams and Eugene wondered what had caused such a no-nonsense outburst from the barman. As they discussed the situation, the barman sent two complimentary drinks over to the blondes, which only further exacerbated the Rams. With that embarrassing episode behind them and, having finally accepted that New York was still nursing a massive Paddy's Day hangover, the lads decided to call it a night, and they returned to their hotels.

The following night Eugene returned to the same bar, the events of the previous night still playing on his mind as his eyes drifted round the premises. Suddenly he spotted a gold-framed photo hung on the wall.

'I don't believe it,' he said, almost dropping his pint to the floor.

There, posing in the photo, were two heavenly *Chanel* models, the very same blondes who had been in the bar 24 hours earlier. After a further bit of investigative work, Eugene discovered that the girls lived less than a block away, and this was their friendly local pub, a place where they expected to be free from sub-standard pickup lines and doe-eyed Munterconnaught men.

Unfortunately, Rams wasn't present for Eugene's big discovery. He was back in Ron's house in Boston, having just arrived by train late that night. The rest of the lads had flown home earlier that day, and now only three days remained before Rams would be doing likewise. He had enjoyed the Big Apple immensely, and in his mind there was no way Boston could top it. But he was wrong, very wrong indeed.

Chapter 34

WHERE EVERYBODY KNOWS YOUR NAME

SUNDAY 23 March 2003. Rams's flight to Dublin would depart Boston's Logan Airport at 7.50pm. It had been a superb nine-day holiday, and the final three days in Boston had given Rams the chance to relax after the excessiveness of Paddy's Day in New York. The parade and related celebrations had brought the Irish out in force on the streets and in the bars of the Big Apple, but Boston was Irish through and through the whole year round. And it wasn't just a case of Americans thinking they were Irish because their great grand-father had been to Cork once. Boston was full of born and bred Irish people. Strong Irish accents abounded everywhere the Rams went, and at times he felt that fun-loving Boston was the city Dublin used to be before people became obsessed with money and property, forget-ting how to have a good time in the process.

Rams and Ron went for breakfast on Sunday morning in an Irish bar in Dorchester and, following a deliciously greasy fry and a couple of sociable pints with some of Ron's friends, it was decided to visit The Littlest Bar on Province Street, which necessitated catching a train into town. The Littlest Bar, however, was worth the trip.

Licensed to hold a mere 38 customers, The Littlest Bar did exactly what it said on the tin. It was tiny; about the size of an average sitting room. Rams had met fellow Munterconnaught man, Paul Hetherton, there the previous night and had enjoyed tremendous banter and craic in the tiny establishment. But Ron was adamant that the bar was even better during the day, so it was time to put that theory to the test. The Littlest Bar was so small that quite often all the customers present would become involved in the same conversation. So predictably, within five minutes of arriving, Rams was in his element, spinning yarns to a captivated audience. Ever since he had attempted to teach Miss Plunkett's class all those years earlier, Rams found he got a great kick out of making people laugh. Over the years he came to realise that he was blessed with a rare talent to do just that and, although some might say he was an attention seeker, few could deny that he was capable of reducing just about anyone to convulsions within minutes of meeting them. And now he was doing what he did best thousands of miles away from home.

Suddenly a voice from the opposite end of the bar piped up.

'Where are ya from?' asked the stranger.

'Cavan. And yourself?' replied the Rams, instantly recognising the accent.

'I'm from Cavan too.'

'Ah right. What part are ya from?' asked the Rams in an attempt to make polite conversation.

'Do you know the way Cavan is shaped like a guitar?' asked Cavan Man.

Rams had never thought of it that way or heard it described as such but, as he pictured the county's shape in his head and realised that Cavan Man's likening of it to a guitar was pretty accurate, he nodded his head in agreement and his neighbour continued the comparison.

'I'm from the part where ya tune the guitar in,' he said. 'What part are you from?'

By now, you could have heard a pin drop in The Littlest Bar as everyone waited with baited breath for Rams's response.

'Well I'm from where the big hole in the guitar is,' he responded without pondering his response for any more than a fraction of a second.

A deafening sound of laughter engulfed the pub. Many of the patrons were Irish ex-pats who seemed to be enjoying the good humoured, uniquely Irish conversation. It gave them a brief reminder of what they missed about Ireland but, at that moment in time, none of them would have dared swap The Littlest Bar for anywhere else in the world. And the show wasn't over yet.

Turning to face Ron, Rams complained about having to catch a flight that evening. He was beginning to love The Littlest Bar, and he didn't want to leave. Cavan Man's ears quickly pricked up.

'What flight are ya on?' he roared.

'The 10 to 8 flight with Aer Lingus,' replied the Rams.

'Jaysis, I'm on the same flight myself,' said Cavan Man, obviously delighted with the news. 'I'll tell ya what. We'll meet up in the airport and go on the beer. And then we'll get the one seat on the plane, the one seat I tell ya.'

'We might want to get more than one seat,' retorted the Rams. 'Ya don't want me sitting on your knee for five or six hours.'

Once again the bar erupted in laughter, and Cavan Man immediately turned his attention back to his pint, unsure as to whether or not Rams was taking the piss out of him.

Rams also took a breather to take a sip from his beer and, in doing so, noticed that a selection of *The Littlest Bar* branded thongs were on sale behind the counter. With only an hour remaining before he would have to depart the premises, he realised that since he already had three drinks lined up in front of him, he'd have to spend his money on something other than alcohol if he was to rid himself of the 70 dollars that remained in his wallet and were weighing him down. The ladies' underwear offered an unorthodox solution.

'Throw us out a pair of knickers there, Horse,' he ordered the bemused barman.

Within 10 minutes Rams had purchased three differently coloured thongs at 10 dollars a pop. Fortunately, he didn't have to wait long to knock some sort of comedy value out of his new possessions.

A middle-aged Irish woman and her three daughters had just entered the premises. As they stood waiting to get served, Rams turned to one of the daughters, a red thong held aloft in his left hand.

'Are these yours?' he asked.

Such toilet humour would probably have resulted in a look of indignation in Dublin. Not so in Boston, however, where it seemed everyone was on happy pills at 4 o'clock on a Sunday afternoon.

'No,' laughed the girl. 'But I'm wearing the exact same pair.'

'No way,' retorted the Rams. 'Prove it.'

With that, the girl unzipped her jeans to reveal *The Littlest Bar* branded underwear. The Rams—never one to miss a genuine opportunity—captured the moment on camera as Ron and his friends looked on in disbelief.

'And what knickers are you wearing?' Rams said cheekily to the prettiest of the sisters.

'Oh, I'm not wearing any,' she replied teasingly.

As Rams attempted to convince the girl to prove to the bar that she was indeed, 'going commando', Cavan Man tried to get the barman's attention. He was obviously impressed with the apparent pulling power of the thongs.

'Five pairs of knickers,' he ordered at the top of his voice.

The barman was now taking in more money in sales of lingerie than in beer, and he was forced to rush to the cellar to source more thongs for the severely depleted shelves.

The craic continued unabated, but for Rams the big adventure was almost over, and it was time to wave goodbye to The Littlest Bar. Leaving Ron and all his new buddies behind, Rams flagged down a taxi, which would have to bring him to Dorchester to collect his bags before heading towards the airport.

'There'll be no tip for this fella,' thought the Rams as the taxi neared Logan Airport. The reason behind Rams's Scrooge-like thinking was because the meter currently read 38 dollars and, due to his needless splurge on knickers, he had only 40 dollars left in his wallet. With Terminal E now in sight, Rams hopped out of the taxi rather than risk running out of money before reaching the front entrance. And besides, he had a funny feeling that the taxi driver wouldn't accept a 10-dollar thong as part payment.

As Rams's mind wandered during the six-hour flight to Ireland, he began thinking about his birthday, which was but six days away. Twenty-five years—a quarter of a century—had passed since Rams first graced this fine planet. Suddenly he realised that he was in his mid-twenties, and he remembered clearly one of his secondary school teachers telling him to, 'grow up a few years', when he was about 17. But Rams had grown up quite a bit since his teens. Most people didn't see it, but he had in some respects matured into a very reflective and thoughtful young man.

Family, close friends, good health and a sense of humour go a long way in this life, but many people don't see the bigger picture these days. They're too busy climbing over each other to build successful careers at the expense of their family and friends. Rams was now at an age where he truly appreciated the true treasures in life that many people take for granted, and he felt privileged to have been raised by two wonderful parents in a little-known magical place called Munterconnaught.

Sure, there's nothing mature about drinking to excess, inventing new words on the fly, giving ridiculous nicknames to people or making a joke about pretty much everything in life, whether appropriate or not. But it sure is fun. We only get one shot at this life and we'll all be a long time dead. So by all means go ahead and work hard to make a living, but work even harder at having a life and, who knows, you might even enjoy yourself. That was Rams's attitude, and it had served him well so far.

'Grow up a few years?' he thought. *'Maybe in another 25 years.'*

ISBN 142516484-6

9 781425 164843